Closing the Deficit

Closing the Deficit

How Much Can Later Retirement Help?

GARY BURTLESS

HENRY J. AARON

Editors

BROOKINGS INSTITUTION PRESS
Washington, D.C.

Library of Congress Cataloging-in-Publication data

Closing the deficit : how much can later retirement help? / Gary Burtless and
Henry J. Aaron, editors.
        pages   cm
    Includes bibliographical references and index.
    ISBN 978-0-8157-0403-4 (pbk. : alk. paper)
        1. Retirement—Government policy—United States.   2. Retirement—
Economic aspects—United States.   3. Budget deficits—United States.
I. Burtless, Gary T., 1950–   II. Aaron, Henry J.
    HQ1063.2.U6C585 2013
    331.25'20973—dc23   2013022756

9 8 7 6 5 4 3 2 1

Printed on acid-free paper

Typeset in Adobe Garamond

Composition by R. Lynn Rivenbark
Macon, Georgia

Printed by R. R. Donnelley
Harrisonburg, Virginia

Contents

Preface

As the proportion of the population that is old has grown in the United States and other industrial countries, policymakers and scholars have devoted increasing attention to the fiscal consequence of aging. To students of government budgets this development is unsurprising. Public programs that provide income and health insurance to the aged are already large and costly. And as elderly populations grow, keeping government affordable will mean keeping the cost of old-age programs affordable.

The essays in this volume examine one approach to this fiscal challenge—increasing the age of retirement. Later retirements could occur because worker preferences change or because public policy encourages people to work until older ages. Since the early 1990s the age at which U.S. workers have left the labor force has risen gradually. The delay in retirement is traceable in part to a shift in public and private pension arrangements. Pension rules and financial incentives that once encouraged workers to exit the workforce before their mid-60s have been eliminated or revised. In addition, workers may have become more aware that increasing life spans mean that they must either save more or work longer to enjoy a comfortable retirement. A gradual shift in social norms may also be conferring greater prestige on workers who exit the labor force at a later age rather than collect pensions at an earlier one.

What would be the budgetary impact if Americans retired later than they currently do? Several of the essays in the volume address this question, directly or indirectly. If workers retire later, their lifetime earnings—and tax payments—are likely to be higher. If current pension rules and formulas remain unchanged, Social Security payments will be delayed. Workers who retire later receive payments for fewer years, but their monthly benefits are increased, so that the lifetime value of benefits will not be reduced. A delay in retirement may also reduce public health insurance benefits received under Medicare.

The first chapters in this book present estimates of the overall impact on the federal budget of a continued increase in retirement ages. Later chapters address the plight of older Americans whose work capacity is limited. How much should we change pension formulas and insurance rules to encourage later retirement? What kind of provision should be made for workers whose health or economic circumstances make it hard to work past 60?

We thank Kathleen Christensen and the Alfred P. Sloan Foundation for encouragement and financial support for the project. Funding was obtained under the Sloan Foundation's Working Longer program, which provides support for research at a number of institutions to "expand and deepen our understanding of aging Americans' work patterns." Since the inception of the project we benefited from crucial contributions from Karen Smith and Richard Johnson of the Urban Institute and Mark Zandi and colleagues at Moody's Analytics. These collaborators helped us develop and test the simulation estimates reported by Smith and Johnson in chapter 3. We are also grateful for the helpful comments and suggestions of the other contributors. Maria Ramrath, Kathleen Burke, Joe Ornstein, Natasha Plotkin, and Jean Marie Callan provided outstanding research assistance. Kathleen Eliot Yinug of Brookings Institution ably organized the conference at which the findings of the research project were first presented. At the Brookings Institution Press, Janet Walker managed editorial matters and Mary Paden edited the final manuscript; Larry Converse handled production, and Susan Woollen oversaw the cover development.

Introduction

GARY BURTLESS AND HENRY AARON

Americans past the age of 60 are delaying their withdrawal from the labor force. This trend is relatively recent and only became detectable in the 1990s. It reverses a century-long trend toward earlier retirement that began in the late nineteenth century. Along with gradually increasing life-expectancy, the historical trend toward early retirement meant that, during the first nine decades of the twentieth century, successive generations of workers spent a growing portion of their lives in retirement.

Since the introduction of Social Security in the 1930s and Medicare and Medicaid in the 1960s, the government has assumed a growing role in providing income and health insurance to the retired elderly. The trend toward earlier retirement increased the budget burden of supporting the aged for two reasons. It reduced the tax payments of the elderly, because retirement income, including social security, is more lightly taxed than earned income. And it increased current government outlays on the aged, because retirees are more likely to need and qualify for public transfers and health insurance than people who continue to work. The reversal of the trend toward earlier retirement almost certainly lessens the budget burden of supporting the aged, but by how much?

This volume summarizes the findings of a project that investigated this question. The researchers did so by answering a related question: How would the budget outlook change if the trend toward *later* retirement accelerated? How much would government revenues grow and how much would outlays shrink if workers on average retired later?

Public and private decision makers have a shared interest in the answer to this question. Although the long-term budget outlook is uncertain, it seems likely the cost of programs for the aged will outpace tax revenues available to pay for them. In view of this budgetary challenge, policymakers and voters should be interested

1

in assessing policies that increase the portion of adult life that people spend in paid employment.

The benefits for taxpayers of such an extension should be clear. If Americans spend an increased fraction of their adult lives earning incomes and supporting themselves, they will need less support in the form of retirement pensions and health benefits. The cost of public provision for old-age income security would be reduced. Past low birth rates and rising longevity, which push up the percentage of the population that is older than the traditional retirement age, raise the budgetary consequences of such a shift. The impending retirement of the baby boom generation, which will boost the fraction of retirees in the population, makes it more urgent to understand the potential impacts of a higher average retirement age on the revenues, outlays, and net budget balance of the government.

The essays in this volume address four kinds of questions about past and future retirement trends and public policies to influence them.

—What kinds of workers have delayed their retirement in the past two decades, and in what way have they extended their work lives?

—How would an increase in the average retirement age, absent any change in public policy, affect the federal budget?

—Can and should public policy be changed to encourage Americans to retire later? What would such measures look like? Whom would they help, and whom would they hurt?

—What companion policies could protect older or impaired workers who find it difficult or impossible to remain employed?

The studies in this book address these questions. They were carried out with generous support from the Alfred P. Sloan Foundation's Working Longer program.

The book begins with two chapters by Gary Burtless. The first describes past trends in labor force participation among older workers. In brief, retirement ages fell throughout most of the twentieth century. That trend stopped in the late 1980s and early 1990s. Over the next two decades, labor force participation rates among older workers rose substantially. Several forces contributed to the increase. The relative importance of each of those forces is difficult to gauge. Better educated workers tend to remain economically active until later ages than do less-well-educated workers; and average education levels of the aged and near-aged increased. In addition, male retirement ages within each education group have also increased. Among women, labor force participation increased among all groups, and this shift reinforced the effect of improved education. The move from defined-benefit pensions, which tend to encourage early retirement, to defined-contribution plans, which are generally neutral in their retirement incentives, also promoted later retirement. Both full- and part-time work increased among elderly and near-elderly workers. Workers with comparatively high earnings were more likely than workers with lower wages to remain in the labor force. There is little evidence to suggest that the growth in work took the form of shifting to less-stressful or temporary "bridge" jobs. Employment in those kinds of jobs increased, but so did continuation in career jobs.

The second chapter presents a scenario under which retirement ages continue to increase. This scenario contrasts with a "baseline projection" prepared by the Social Security actuaries for the 2011 Social Security Trustees' report, the "The 2011 Annual Report of the Board of Trustees of the Federal Old-Age and Survivors Insurance and Federal Disability Insurance Trust Funds." The trustees' projections are based on the assumption that the trend toward later retirement, which began in the late 1980s and early 1990s, will dramatically slow or end. In contrast, Burtless creates an alternative scenario in which the trend of the past two decades toward later retirement continues more or less unchanged through 2040. As a result, he projects a larger future labor force than the Social Security Trustees forecast in their report. The larger labor force means that potential gross domestic product (GDP) *at full employment* can be larger than the trustees predict. A larger GDP means greater tax collections—through higher payroll taxes, personal income taxes, and corporation income taxes. Delays in retirement would also mean that pension expenditures are delayed. Both developments improve the government's budget prospects.

The analytical challenge is to estimate the size of the increase in GDP and of the positive impact on budget balance. That impact depends on how much the additional workers add to national output and taxes and how long pension benefits are delayed, which in turn depends on the characteristics of the workers who are predicted to remain economically active. The third chapter deals with this analytical challenge. Its authors, Karen Smith and Richard Johnson, use the Urban Institute's Dynamic Simulation of Income Model (DYNASIM) to identify which workers would be most likely to remain economically active if labor force participation among older age groups increased. Because well-educated people with comparatively high earning potential tend to remain economically active in the baseline forecast, Smith and Johnson predict that the big changes in behavior will occur in the bottom half of the earnings distribution.

To estimate the impact on national output of this increase in the workforce, the project contracted with Moody's Econometrics, a macroeconomic forecasting firm. Its goal was to make plausible projections of future GDP and employment, taking into account the reality that many people who wish to hold jobs will be unable to find them. In developing a macroeconomic projection for the baseline scenario, Moody's task was made easier by the fact that its own forecast was adjusted to conform with the Social Security Trustees' forecast of future GDP and employment. Creating an alternative projection in which the desired labor force participation rate of the aged is higher represented a more formidable challenge. When the analysis was performed, the U.S. economy had not fully recovered from the deep recession that began in 2008. Under these circumstances, an increase in the labor force that makes more people available for work would not necessarily translate into additional employment. As long as demand is inadequate to generate enough jobs for the current labor force, an increase in the number of labor force participants will result in a much bigger increase in the number of unemployed than in the number of employed. If labor supply increases and not all workers can immediately find employment, it is necessary to develop a sound basis for identifying which workers will find work and which ones will remain jobless.

There is no single best solution to these analytical challenges. The solution we adopted was to prepare three projections of future employment change when there is inadequate overall demand for workers. Under first scenario, Moody's and Smith and Johnson assume that the unemployment rate immediately falls to a level deemed consistent with full employment, thus absorbing the increased number of aged and near-aged assumed to enter the labor force. This scenario is unrealistic, but it shows the full increase in potential GDP, taxes, and earnings that would result from an increase in desired labor supply among the aged. Smith and Johnson identify which older Americans will attempt to join the labor force based on workers' observable characteristics and work histories. Those identified as joining the workforce have characteristics and previous behavior that put them closest to the margin of working. The workers who defer retirement in this scenario will not have the same characteristics—earnings levels and productivity—as those who are in the labor force in the baseline. As noted above, workers who are comparatively well educated and well paid tend to work until later ages in the baseline than do those with low wages and education. Consequently, the average productivity, contribution to GDP, and earnings of the added workers will on average be lower than those of workers who are employed in the baseline.

Under the two other scenarios, the economy is assumed to recover gradually, returning to full employment during or shortly after 2017. Until full employment is achieved, it is necessary to specify which members of the enlarged labor force will find work and which will be unemployed. In both these scenarios Smith and Johnson rely on Moody's macroeconomic forecast to determine the total number of additional labor force participants who will find jobs. Actual employment gains are limited by the future path of aggregate demand. As long as demand is depressed, too few workers will find work to attain full employment. Under one scenario, Smith and Johnson assume that all the additional unemployment caused by the increase in old-age labor force participation will be divided among participants who are 55 or older, the subpopulation predicted to have increased labor supply. Under the other scenario, Smith and Johnson assume the added unemployment resulting from higher old-age participation rates has spillover effects on the unemployment of younger workers. The additions to unemployment are "shared" among the young and the old.

After 2018, when full employment is assumed to be achieved, there is little difference among the projections generated by the three scenarios. The labor force participation rate of the aged is higher than it is in the baseline forecast, which is derived from the Social Security Trustees' projections, but the overall unemployment among young and old is the same as it is in the baseline projection.

The simulations by Smith and Johnson and Moody's Econometrics, based on Burtless's labor force projections, suggest that by 2040 the U.S. labor force would be more than 3 percent larger than projected by the Social Security Administration. The biggest percentage increases are projected to occur among workers in their late 60s and early 70s. Labor force participation among some age groups will rise by roughly one third. As a result, earnings increase substantially, particularly among people near the bottom of the income distribution, few of whom are economically active in the baseline. The increase in work and earnings boosts government revenues during the simulation period by more than $2 trillion and lowers expenditures on Social Security and Medicare by more than $600 billion. Higher revenues and lower spending reduce government debt and associated interest payments. Overall, the simulations indicate that government debt would be lower by more than $4 trillion if the labor force expanded by as much as Burtless's projections indicate.

Whether such savings comprise a large or a small *proportion* of any future budget gap obviously depends on the size of the gap. The Congressional Budget Office (CBO) publishes two long-term budget projections. Under its "Extended Baseline" projection, the ratio of federal government debt to GDP remains relatively stable through 2040. Under CBO's "Alternative Budget Scenario," deficits grow rapidly and the ratio of debt to GDP grows explosively. Compared with CBO's Extended Baseline projection, the savings shown in the Smith-Johnson simulations represent a sizeable fraction of the projected deficit in 2040. In contrast, the savings have a negligible proportional impact on the huge growth of debt under CBO's Alternative Budget Scenario. Thus, whether one believes the impact of delayed retirement is significant from the standpoint of the budget depends on one's view of the likely future course of the deficit. If one is pessimistic about future budget prospects, the changes to future revenues and outlays that would be caused by later retirement only marginally affect the outlook. If one is optimistic and accepts CBO's Extended Baseline forecast, the changes are much more significant. Under CBO's Extended Baseline projection, however, the government's long-term deficit does not appear to be a serious problem.

In comments on the analytical findings, Eugene Steuerle expresses the view that the actual increase in the labor force would likely be even larger than Burtless's projections indicate. He notes that past projections of employment by the Social Security Administration (SSA) have underestimated the increase in employment among older workers. When the relative supply of younger workers declines as a result of earlier drops in fertility, Steuerle argues, employers will increase their demand for older workers and improve the attractiveness of work for this group. Thus, the positive impact on public budgets and the incomes of older workers (especially those who otherwise would have low incomes) could be considerably larger than the Smith-Johnson simulations indicate.

Joyce Manchester of the Congressional Budget Office notes that CBO has already increased its projections of future labor supply in comparison to those made by the SSA. In fact, the current CBO assumptions about future labor supply lie roughly half-way between their former levels—which were similar to those from the SSA that Smith and Johnson used in their baseline projections—and the alternative forecast supplied by Burtless. Thus, CBO has already incorporated into its own projections much of the fiscal gain shown in the Smith-Johnson simulations.

Manchester also points out that the gradual increase in the age at which Social Security pays unreduced benefits has had a demonstrable impact on the ages at which workers actually claim benefits. That said, more workers continue to claim retirement benefits as soon as they can, at age 62, than claim benefits at the age when Social Security pays unreduced benefits. This finding underscores the potential for changes in public policy to boost labor supply among older workers.

The second part of the book addresses potential policy changes. In chapter 4, Henry Aaron reviews a number of policy changes that have been widely discussed in recent years and presents one new one. Previously introduced changes include across-the-board benefits cuts (often misleadingly described as "raising the retirement age"), raising the age at which retirement benefits may first be claimed, and combining these two changes. These reforms would reduce current benefit payments and thereby contribute to near-term deficit reduction. The expenditure reductions would be permanent in the case of across-the-board benefit cuts. Raising the age of initial eligibility is not an across-the-board benefit cut. Although workers who otherwise would claim retirement benefits at age 62 would be forced to delay benefit claiming to a later age, they would be fully compensated for the delay by collecting larger monthly checks after benefits begin. Thus, the increase in the early entitlement age would cut spending only temporarily. Because expected lifespans have lengthened and interest rates are exceptionally low, the adjustment factor currently used to compensate workers for delayed benefit claiming probably raises the lifetime value of benefits for the average worker.

By reducing pensions or delaying their availability, most proposed reforms would impose hardships on workers for whom continued work would be difficult or impossible. Accordingly, analysts have long sought measures that would offset such hardships by providing targeted protections to those who are particularly vulnerable. Such "safety valves" include liberalized access to Social Security Disability Insurance (SSDI) (for example, by relaxing the current requirement that disability insurance recipients must have worked in five of the most recent ten years) or eased access to Supplemental Security Income (SSI) based on either relaxed disability standards or increased thresholds in income and asset tests. Alternatively, benefit cuts could be imposed only on workers with relatively high average lifetime earnings. One variant of this kind of reform is "progressive indexing," under which benefits would be reduced increasingly over time for successive retiree cohorts but only for workers who had comparatively high average lifetime earnings.

Aaron suggests a new way to encourage later retirement—allowing workers to continue to claim Social Security benefits as early as age 62 but cutting benefits only for early retirees with comparatively high earnings.

The increase in the number of people receiving Social Security disability benefits, the persistently low rates of exit from the disability–insurance program, and the lengthy and expensive process by which people are found eligible for benefits have all led to a sense that the SSDI program needs a thoroughgoing reexamination and overhaul. The fact that the Disability Insurance Trust Fund is projected to be exhausted in 2016 virtually guarantees such scrutiny. Because the average age at which people are being found eligible for disability benefits is falling, the payoff to finding ways to help people recover earning capacity or maintain residual earning capacity is increasing.

Three discussants offer comments on the policies described in Aaron's chapter and present ideas of their own. Nicole Maestas remarks that one's ranking of various policies to encourage later retirement depends in large part on the reasons why one seeks to extend working lives. Is early retirement bad for the budget, bad for workers themselves, or a reflection of poorly designed disability policy? How one answers those questions helps determine which policy changes appear most attractive.

As evidence of the difficulty of determining who is disabled, she presents evidence that the health status is similar among those who file successful claims for disability insurance and those whose applications for benefits are unsuccessful. She also points out that one development contributing to later retirement—the increase in the education level of successive birth cohorts—is winding down, as increases in the education levels of successive age groups are slowing. But the impact on retirement decisions from the changed structure of pensions could continue to increase because most workers who have been affected by the shift from defined-benefit to defined-contribution pension plans are still working.

Richard Burkhauser notes that actions must be taken at some point to close the projected long-term deficit in Social Security and that such changes can be structured to encourage workers to retire later. Rising life expectancy, he argues, justifies ending the early-retirement option under Social Security. This shift in policy would seriously hurt only a small fraction of those who now claim such benefits, namely those whose health is poor and who have access to few other sources of income. The way to support this group, Burkhauser maintains, is through income- or means-tested benefits.

Burkhauser also proposes shifting the way in which the Social Security benefit formula is adjusted over time. The formula for initial pension benefits is currently adjusted based on the annual growth of economywide average earnings. This policy tends to hold roughly constant the ratio of average benefits to average earnings. As real earnings rise, so does the real value of pensions. Burkhauser proposes adjusting the formula based on the annual change in prices. This policy would hold constant the *real* value of pensions. As real earnings rise, the ratio of pensions to earnings would gradually fall. The savings from such a change could be better used, he argues, to raise benefits in such means-tested programs as SSI.

Debra Whitman stresses that the major policy challenge to advocates of curtailing benefits for those who retire early is to identify ways to protect those for whom retirement is more a necessity than a choice. She emphasizes that the increase in life expectancy that many cite as a justification for raising the age of initial eligibility for Social Security or for cutting benefits is not evenly distributed. High earners have experienced large increases in life expectancy, but low earners have not. For that reason, basing policy reform on population averages can do unintended harm. She also draws attention to the political obstacles to increasing access to SSI. Aged and disabled adults who become entitled to SSI automatically become eligible for Medicaid, which imposes heavy fiscal burdens on states. She also urges policymakers to draw lessons from behavioral economics, which has shown that seemingly minor shifts in choice frameworks, or "nudges," can materially influence behavior. Because early retirement is, in fact, often an economically unwise decision given that it entails a permanent reduction in benefits, such nudges could significantly improve welfare. She singles out one change in Social Security for criticism: the proposal to adjust currently payable benefits based on a new price index that increases more slowly than the one now used to adjust benefits. Such a shift, she argues, would impose gradually increasing burdens the longer that people are on the rolls—a serious matter for the very old and the long-term disabled.[1]

The volume concludes with a chapter by John Shoven and comments by Steve Pearlstein. Shoven challenges the notion that people are now retiring when they are "older" than workers who retired twenty years ago. If age is measured not by years-since-birth, but by years-until-death, people retiring now are no older than they were two decades ago, because average life expectancy has increased as much as the average age of retirement. More basically, Shoven points out that given current life expectancies and typical ages of retirement—64 for men and 62 for women—spouses can expect to work for perhaps forty years and will spend an average of about twenty-eight years in retirement until both spouses have died. This mix, Shoven points out, requires that more than one-third of lifetime consumption will occur during retirement if living standards are relatively constant throughout life. That arithmetic fact, in turn, requires that something approaching half of their earnings must be saved in one form or another by active workers to support retirement living standards. The savings can occur through individual savings or group pensions, private or public. In any case, Shoven suggests that such saving rates or transfer payments will be highly problematic and may prove impossible to sustain.

For this reason, Shoven argues, the trend toward later retirements will and must continue. He proposes two specific policies to encourage such trends. The first policy would excuse workers with forty years of employment and their employers from having to pay payroll taxes for Social Security and Medicare. Such workers would be treated as "paid up." The tax relief would be considerable, as payroll taxes are levied at a rate of 12.4 percent for Social Security on earnings up to $113,700 and at 2.9 percent for Medicare on earnings up to $200,000 for individuals and $250,000 for couples and 4.7 percent on earnings above these thresholds. Depending on adjustments in wages that might occur because of a cut in payroll taxes after forty years of work, either take-home pay for workers would increase or the cost to employers of hiring older workers would fall. This policy should boost employers' demand for older workers and increase workers' willingness to remain in the labor force.

Shoven's second proposed policy would make Medicare the primary insurer for all workers who are Medicare eligible. Under current law, Medicare covers only the cost of medical care that is not covered by private, employer-sponsored health insurance (unless the employer has fewer than 20 employees). Under the policy

1. Whitman was referring to the particular measure of price change that is used to give annual cost-of-living adjustments to Social Security beneficiaries who are currently collecting a benefit. This differs from the indexing change proposed by Richard Burkhauser, who suggested a reform in the indexing formula used to determine pensioners' *initial* Social Security benefit.

Shoven proposes, Medicare would be the first payer and an employer's private insurance would cover only those services that are included in private coverage but not in Medicare. Because health costs for older workers are several times higher than those of younger workers, this policy shift would considerably lower the relative cost to employers of hiring and retaining older workers.

Shoven also draws attention to calculations showing that most workers would be well advised to delay claiming Social Security as long as possible. The reason is twofold. By waiting to claim Social Security workers receive a larger fully inflation-indexed annuity that is completely safe. No private asset has all of these attractive features. Furthermore, the price of this annuity is lower than that of any privately available annuity. The cost of claiming "too early" can exceed $200,000 in some cases. Although waiting is usually the better financial strategy, more workers claim benefits as soon as they are eligible than at any other age, and more than 80 percent claim before age 66. Helping workers understand the value of waiting to claim benefits may also nudge them into a decision to work a bit longer than most do now.

Steve Pearlstein questions whether it would be in the public interest to shrink payroll tax revenues and boost Medicare liabilities through the policy changes that Shoven proposes. The budget is in deficit, and both Social Security and Medicare currently have too little future revenue to cover their long-term obligations. Shoven replies in later discussion that if the policies induced as many people to work as current estimates of the labor supply elasticity of older workers suggest, then the added payroll and income tax revenues from increased national output would offset the direct revenue loss. Pearlstein also warns against assuming that jobs would materialize for the increased labor supply resulting from deferred retirement. However, he joins Shoven in concluding that increased life expectancies virtually require later retirement ages. Without them, the implied transfers from workers to retirees would be problematic. Even more important than these financial questions, he suggests, are the preferences of the elderly themselves. Drawing on Gary Burtless's and Eugene Steuerle's observations about past increases in labor supply and the likelihood they would continue, Pearlstein observes that markets seem to be working reasonably well and suggests that perhaps the best course for public policy would be to stay neutral, neither discouraging nor actively encouraging extended working lives.

1

Who Is Delaying Retirement? Analyzing the Increase in Employment among Older Workers

GARY BURTLESS

Americans past age 60 are delaying their withdrawal from the workforce. This development reverses a trend toward early retirement that lasted longer than a century. The trend toward earlier labor force exit came to an end for U.S. men between the mid-1980s and mid-1990s.[1] After reaching a low point in the 1985–95 decade, the labor force participation rate of 60–64-year-old men has increased more than 6 percentage points (about one-eighth), and the participation rate among 65–69-year-old men has increased about 13 percentage points (more than half). Participation rates among American women in the same age groups have increased even faster, especially when the change is measured in proportional terms.

One explanation for this reversal is the change in incentives for work in later life, a result of reforms in the U.S. Social Security system, the gradual evolution of the nation's employer-based pension system, and the increasing expense of health insurance outside employer-provided group plans. Compared with the 1970s and early 1980s, Social Security retirement benefits now provide fewer and smaller disincentives to work after workers reach the benefit-claiming age. Employer-sponsored retirement plans are now more likely to offer defined-contribution pensions rather than defined-benefit pensions. The latter type of plan can create powerful incentives for workers to leave career jobs after they have attained the earliest benefit-claiming age. In contrast, defined-contribution plans provide stronger incentives for older workers to keep working. Finally, the elimination of many employer-funded retiree health plans combined with steep

The author is grateful to Maria Ramrath, formerly of Brookings, for outstanding research assistance.
1. Burtless and Quinn (2001 and 2002); Bosworth and Burtless (2011).

increases in the cost of health insurance has made it riskier for workers too young for Medicare to leave jobs that provide a health plan.[2]

The goal of this chapter is to identify the groups in successive birth cohorts that have delayed their retirement in the era since the retirement age began to rise. It aims to answer a handful of questions about the trend toward later job exit in the past quarter century: How big is the delay in retirement compared with job exit patterns observed in the late 1980s? Do groups delaying retirement earn above-average wages? Do the workers retiring at later ages have more schooling than average, or do they have below-average educational credentials? Does later retirement primarily take the form of part-time work, or have aged workers also seen an increase in full-time employment? Have older workers delayed their departure from their career jobs? Or have they taken "bridge jobs" that have less responsibility, fewer hours, or worse pay than their previous jobs?

The analysis was performed using Current Population Survey (CPS), which provides detailed monthly data on the labor force status of adults in approximately 60,000 households every month.[3] The available monthly files cover 1977 to the present. During the first decade of the period, the average retirement age declined; during the most recent two and a half decades, the average age at retirement has increased. Each section of this chapter addresses one of the questions mentioned earlier. The chapter concludes with a summary of findings.

How Much Has Workforce Participation Increased at Older Ages?

At the beginning of the twentieth century, retirement was uncommon but not unknown. Just one out of three men past age 65 was outside the paid workforce.[4] By 1950 retirement was more common. Only about 46 percent of men 65 and older held a job or were actively seeking work. The labor force participation rate of aged men continued to decline and reached a low point in 1991, when less than 16 percent of men over 65 were employed or actively seeking a job. The proportion of women over 65 who were employed also fell during much of the twentieth century, but the reduction was far smaller than among men because the percentage of older women in paid work had always been modest.

Changes in Age-Specific Participation Rates

The decline followed by the increase in participation rates among aged Americans in the post–World War II era can be clearly seen in the Bureau of Labor Sta-

---

2. Burtless and Quinn (2001). See also Anderson, Gustman, and Steinmeier (1999).
3. The Current Population Survey, performed by the U.S. Census Bureau for the U.S. Bureau of Labor Statistics, is the primary source of labor force statistics for the population of the United States.
4. U.S. Department of Commerce, Bureau of the Census (1975).

tistics (BLS) estimates of labor force behavior over the past six decades (see appendix table A-1). The statistics for people 65 and older can be somewhat misleading, however, because the ages they cover include both 65–74-year-olds, who tend to have higher workforce participation rates, and people who are past age 75, nearly all of whom have left the workforce. The percentage of the older population in the labor force is affected by both age-specific participation rates and the age profile of elderly Americans. As survival rates have improved, the number of people living past 75 has increased. Conversely, the entry of the large baby boom generation into its retirement years is temporarily increasing the proportion of the aged population that is older than 65 but younger than 75. To eliminate the effect of the changing age composition of the elderly population, we can examine the trend in labor force participation rates at specific ages. Figure 1-1 shows participation rates at ages 60, 62, 65, and 68 during the forty-five years after 1965. The figure shows participation rates for women and men, respectively. The tabulations, performed by the BLS based on monthly CPS data, show a decline in participation rates through the early to mid-1980s among women and a drop through the early 1990s among men. For both men and women, participation rates have increased in the past two decades. They have also increased by proportionately larger amounts at older ages. Among 68-year-old men, for example, the participation rate increased by more than half between 1991 and 2010. Among 68-year-old women, the participation rate increased by about two-thirds.

The estimates of male participation rates in figure 1-1 can be compared with those of Ransom, Sutch, and Williamson (1991) for 1910, derived from the decennial census for that year. Between 1910 and 1991 there were sizeable drops in male participation rates at ages 60, 62, 65, and 68. At age 65, for example, the male participation rate shrank 46 percentage points, falling from 77 percent in 1910 to 31 percent in 1991. At age 60, the male participation rate continued to decline, although very slightly, after 1991. At ages 62, 65, and 68, however, participation rates have rebounded since 1991, erasing about one-quarter of the participation-rate drop that had occurred between 1910 and 1991. Participation rates at older ages remain far below their levels at the beginning of the twentieth century, but at ages past 62, participation rates have increased substantially above the low point they reached in the early 1990s.

Persistence in the Labor Force

Another way to interpret age-specific participation rate trends over time is to calculate the rate at which workers who were in the labor force in a given year and at a given age (say, age 57) remain in the workforce at successively higher ages. For example, men who were age 57 in 1972 had a labor force participation rate of

Figure 1-1. *Labor Force Participation Rates at Selected Ages, 1965–2010*

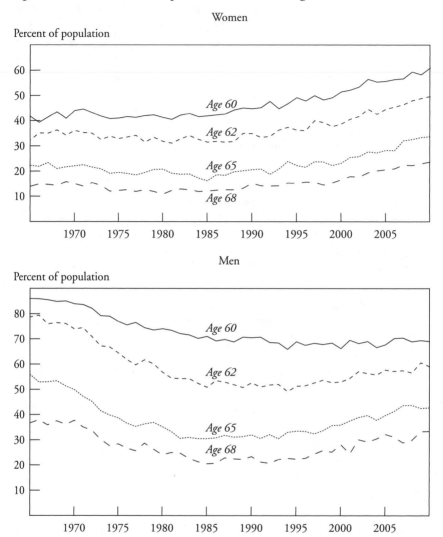

Women

Percent of population

Men

Percent of population

Source: U.S. Bureau of Labor Statistics tabulations of monthly Current Population Survey files.

about 87 percent. When they attained age 62 in 1977, men in this cohort had a participation rate of 60 percent, or about 68 percent of their participation rate when they were 57. By age 65 their participation rate fell to 35 percent, or just four-tenths of their participation rate when they were 57. I define the ratio of a cohort's participation rate at ages over 57 to their participation rate at age 57 as an indicator of the cohort's labor force "persistence" at the later age. A higher rate of persistence at a given age after 57 indicates a slower rate of exit from the labor force.

I estimated cohort labor force participation persistence rates at successive ages between 60 and 80 separately for women and men. Figure 1-2 shows my estimates for four cohorts of workers for ages 62 through 74. The estimates were obtained using BLS-supplied tabulations of monthly CPS files covering calendar years 1976–2010.[5] For each calendar year, BLS analysts calculated the participation rate for persons at each year of age between 60 and 80. The cohort persistence rate at a given age is simply the participation rate at that age measured as a percentage of the participation rate of persons in the cohort when the cohort was 57 years old. The second part of figure 1-2 shows the results of these calculations for four cohorts of men. The oldest cohort was age 60 in 1975; the youngest was 60 in 2005. The other two cohorts were 60 in 1985 and 1995, respectively. Each line in the chart shows the rate of labor force withdrawal of a cohort at successive years of age from 62 through 74. For example, when the youngest male cohort was 62 years old, the participation rate of men in that cohort was 74 percent of the participation rate of the cohort when it was 57 years old (see figure 1-2). At age 63, the participation rate of this same cohort was 70 percent of the cohort's participation rate when it was 57 years old. Not surprisingly, the participation rate of a cohort generally falls in successive years. For the youngest cohorts, I display only four years of labor force persistence rates, because persistence rates in the fifth and later years could not be calculated with data available when the calculations were performed.

The crucial point in figure 1-2 is that labor force persistence has increased in recent cohorts compared with earlier ones. For example, in the oldest male cohort, which was 60 in 1975, the participation rate at age 66 was 33 percent of the cohort's participation rate at age 57. In the male cohort that was 60 in 1995, the participation rate at age 66 was 43 percent of the cohort's participation rate at age 57. Thus the participation rate fell considerably more slowly between ages 57 and 66 for the younger cohort compared with the older one. The persistence rates through age 65 for the cohort that attained 60 in 2005 suggest that this trend continues and, in fact, has become more pronounced between ages 62 and 65. The results in figure 1-2 imply that men who are in the labor force in their late 50s are now leaving the workforce at a slower pace than twenty years ago. In other words, the younger cohort is more persistent in remaining in the labor force. The same pattern of delayed retirement is evident among women (see figure 1-2);

5. As an approximation of a cohort's participation rate at age 57, I used the BLS estimate of the average labor force participation rate (LFPR) for persons between ages 55–59 in the years the cohort was 56, 57, and 58 years old. The BLS has published estimates of participation rates for 55–59-year-olds for years before 1976.

Figure 1-2. *Labor Force Persistence Rates at Indicated Ages for Birth Cohorts Attaining Age 60 in 1975, 1985, 1995, and 2005*

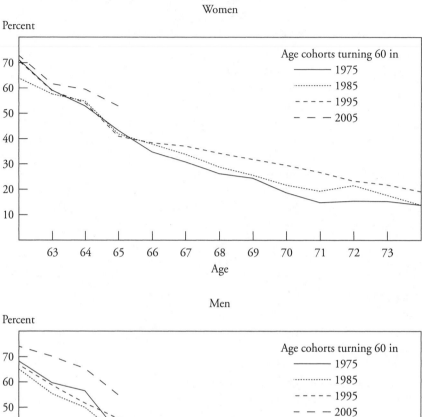

Women

Percent

Men

Percent

Source: Author's calculations based on U.S. Bureau of Labor Statistics tabulations of monthly Current Population Survey files.

Note: The labor force persistence rate at a given age is the cohort's labor force participation rate at that age divided by its estimated labor force participation rate when the birth cohort was 57 years old.

recent cohorts have been more persistent in remaining in the workforce than was common two decades ago.

Figure 1-3 shows how much labor force persistence has increased at various ages between 60 and 79. I have calculated the increase in the participation rate at successive ages measured as a percent of the cohort's participation rate at age 57. The calculations are performed at individual ages between 60 and 79. After tabulating the persistence rates in 1988–90 and 2008–10, I calculated the increase in persistence at the indicated ages between the two sets of years. (I averaged the persistence rates for three years at the start and the end of the analysis period to reduce the impact of year-to-year variability in measuring cohorts' persistence rates.) The top panel in figure 1-3 shows the increased persistence of old-age labor-force participation among women. The bottom panel shows the same set of results for men. For both women and men, the trends in persistence are comparable. The increase in persistence is modest at ages 60 and 61, peaks at age 65, remains relatively high through age 72, and then declines. Except at ages 60 to 61 and 77 to 79, the increase in labor force persistence has been greater among men than among women.

Do Workers Postponing Retirement Earn Below-Average Wages?

The tabulations in figures 1-1 through 1-3 show unambiguously that both labor force participation and the persistence of labor force engagement has increased in the past quarter century. The statistics do not, however, shed any light on the kinds of workers who are postponing retirement. The next two sections attempt to provide some answers to this question. This section shows how the relative wages of the older working population have changed over time. I focus on wage and salary earners who are 62 years old or older, because these are the older workers who have seen the largest proportionate increases in participation and labor force persistence (see figure 1-3).

To perform the analysis, I estimated the age profile of hourly wages separately for calendar years 1985–91 and 2004–10 using wage data reported in the monthly outgoing rotation group (ORG) CPS files.[6] The files contain about 25,000 worker records per month, or approximately 300,000 per calendar year. Given the large sample size, it is possible to estimate average and median earnings within narrow age groups. I divided each year's 25-to-74-year-old male and female samples into nine five-year age groups plus two age groups—60–61 and 62–64—that separate people in their early 60s on the basis of their potential eligibility for Social Security retired

6. Schmitt (2003).

Figure 1-3. *Increase in Persistence in the Labor Force of Women and Men Aged 60–79, 1988–90 to 2008–10*

Women

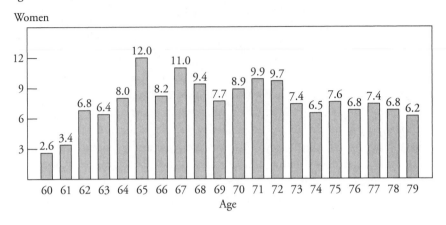

Men

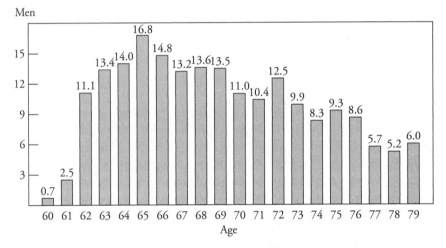

Source: Author's calculations based on U.S. BLS tabulations of monthly CPS files, as explained in text.
Note: A birth cohort's labor force participation rate at age 57 is calculated as the arithmetic average of the participation rates of 55–59-year-olds in the calendar years when the cohort was 56, 57, and 58 years old.

worker benefits. The first seven years of the analysis period, 1985–91, represent the final years of the trend toward early retirement. The last seven years, 2004–10, represent recent years in which old-age labor force participation rates have rebounded. Even though the second period includes one of the worst recessions since World War II, the average unemployment rates in the two sets of years are similar. The civilian unemployment rate averaged 6.2 percent between 1985 and 1991 and 6.4 percent between 2004 and 2010.

Table 1-1. *Increase in Effective Labor Supply of Older U.S. Workers, 1985–91 and 2004–10*

	Age group		
Cohort	62–64	65–69	70–74
Women			
Change in			
Labor force participation rate (percentage points)	13.2	10.1	6.4
Employment-population ratio	12.4	9.5	6.0
Percent of population	12.0	9.0	5.5
At work, percent of population in			
Full-time employment	7.4	5.2	2.5
Part-time employment	5.0	4.4	3.5
Men			
Change in			
Labor force participation rate (percentage points)	7.4	9.1	6.9
Employment-population ratio	6.5	8.2	6.4
Percent of population	7.0	8.1	6.1
At work, percent of population in			
Full-time employment	2.4	6.2	4.1
Part-time employment	4.1	2.0	2.3

Source: Author's tabulations of monthly CPS files for 1985–91 and 2004–10.

Table 1-1 shows estimates of the change in a variety of indicators of women's and men's old-age labor supply between 1985–91 and 2004–10. (These estimates were derived from tabulations of *all* the monthly CPS files in 1985–91 and 2004–10 rather than just the ORG files.) Labor supply changes are shown separately for women and men between ages 62–64, 65–69, and 70–74. In the nearly two decades between the two sets of estimates, labor force participation rates increased between 6.4 and 13.2 percentage points in the case of older women and increased between 6.9 and 9.1 percentage points in the case of older men. The other indicators of labor supply increased in these age groups as well, and the increases were proportionately as large, relative to baseline labor supply, as the increases in labor force participation.

Figure 1-4 shows the age profiles of relative hourly earnings in the two sets of years. In each narrow age group, the average wage is measured relative to the mean wage of women or men who are between 35 and 54 years old. Clearly, the relative hourly earnings of older women and men have improved compared with those of prime-age workers. In all three of the older age groups, women's hourly wages in 1985–91 were below the average wages earned by 35-to-54-year-olds. In 2004–10 they remained below the average hourly wage of 35-to-54-year-old women, but the discrepancy was significantly smaller. The improvement in relative wages of 62-to-74-year-old women was about 8 percent. The improvement in older men's relative earnings compared with 35-to-54-year-old men was even greater (see lower panel of figure 1-4). In all three of the older age groups, men's hourly wages in the earlier period were below the average wages earned by 35-to-54-year-old men. By 2004–10 earnings of 62-to-64-year-olds were slightly higher than those of 35-to-54-year-old men, and the earnings of 65-to-74-year-olds were much closer to the hourly wages of 35-to-54-year-olds. The relative earnings of older men improved 8 percent among 62-to-64-year-olds, 20 percent among 65-to-69-year-olds, and 26 percent among men between 70 and 74. Thus, the increase in the labor supply of older workers was accompanied by an improvement rather than a decline in their relative hourly wages.[7]

Are Workers Who Postpone Retirement Better Educated than Average?

One reason that the average hourly pay of older workers has improved compared with that of prime-age workers is that older workers are now relatively better educated than older workers in the past. Among male wage earners between 62 and 74, the proportion who have graduated from college increased about one-seventh between 1985–91 and 2004–10 and the fraction who failed to complete high school fell about one-fifth. The improvement in educational credentials among older female workers was smaller but still impressive. The gains in college education and the drop in the proportion of older workers who are high school dropouts are relatively larger than the changes seen among prime-age workers. Thus, some of the relative wage gains of older workers are traceable to the fact that gains in schooling among prime-age workers were smaller between 1985–91 and 2004–10 than they were among workers who are between 62 and 74 years old. In part this reflects the rapid gains in schooling attainment that occurred after World War II, when people who are now 62 to 74 years old were enrolled in secondary school and college. In some measure it also reflects the divergence between retirement patterns among older Americans with good educational credentials and those who have less schooling.

Before presenting evidence on differences in retirement patterns by educational attainment, it is worth noting that the wages of older workers have

7. Between 1985 and 2010 the BLS modified the top-coding of wages in the CPS ORG files, and the revised top-coding procedures may affect the trends in mean wages displayed in figure 1-4. To investigate this possibility, I re-estimated the age-earnings profile using median wage earnings rather than mean earnings. The basic results do not differ from those in figure 1-4. Notwithstanding the increase in old-age labor supply, wage earners past age 62 experienced a relative improvement in their median pay between 1985–91 and 2004–10.

Figure 1-4. *Age Profiles of Hourly Wages, 1985–91 and 2004–10*

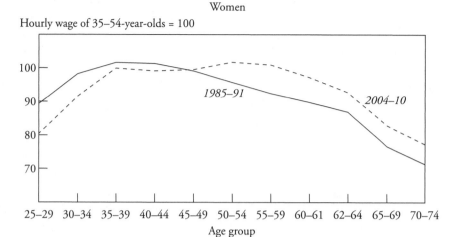

Women

Hourly wage of 35–54-year-olds = 100

1985–91

2004–10

Age group

Men

Hourly wage of 35–54-year-olds = 100

2004–10

1985–91

Age group

Source: Author's tabulations of monthly 1985–91 and 2004–10 outgoing rotation group (ORG) from Current Population Survey files.

improved compared with those earned by prime-age workers, even accounting for the relative improvement in older workers' schooling. To show this, I separately estimated the age-earnings profiles of women and men in four educational groups—those without a high school diploma, those with a high school degree but no schooling after high school, those with some college education who have not obtained a four-year degree, and those who have completed at least four years of college. (The last group also includes college graduates who have obtained a post-college degree.) With only a handful of exceptions, these tabulations show that older wage earners *within* each educational group have seen relative improvements in their wages compared with younger workers. The only notable exceptions are college graduates between 62 and 64 years old, who saw a modest decline in their wages compared with younger college graduates. Among college graduates 65 and older, there were noticeable improvements in the relative wages of older workers compared with prime-age workers. On balance, this analysis suggests that older workers in every educational category have enjoyed relative wage gains compared with their younger educational peers, despite the fact that a greater percentage of older workers is staying in the workforce until later in life.

In general, workers who are better educated tend to remain in the workforce longer than workers in the same birth cohorts who have less schooling. This was true in the early period, 1985–91, as well as in the most recent period, 2004–10. However, the labor participation gap between less educated and more educated older Americans has widened over the past two decades. In 1985–91, for example, 65–69-year-old married men with a college degree had a 15-percentage-point edge in workforce participation compared with married men the same age who had only a high school diploma. In the same period, 65–69-year-old married men who failed to complete high school had a 5-percentage-point shortfall in participation compared with married high school graduates in their age group. Among older married women, the educational gradient of labor force participation was similar to that among older married men, though the observed differences between educational groups were a bit smaller.

The increasing educational attainment of older Americans should therefore be expected to boost participation rates among 62–74-year-olds, even if there were no trend toward later retirement among Americans holding constant their educational attainment. Statistical analysis shows, however, that labor force participation rose within the great majority of marital status and education groups in the older population. Thus, participation increased in older age groups *both* because the older population became relatively more educated *and* because older Americans with the same schooling levels tended to postpone their age of exit from the workforce.

Table 1-2 shows changes in labor force participation rates between 1985–91 and 2004–10 within demographic cells defined by older Americans' gender, marital status, educational attainment, and age group. The results were obtained from separate regressions for women and men using the monthly CPS files for 1985–91 and 2004–10. The regression specification for each gender includes the main effects of principal demographic factors—exact year of age, race, educational attainment group, and marital status—as well as seasonal adjustment factors and the seasonally adjusted monthly unemployment rate of adults between

25 and 54. The coefficients are estimated using the linear probability model and reflect the effects of educational attainment and marital status on the average *change* in participation rates between 1985–91 and 2004–10. With few exceptions the statistically significant coefficients are positive, indicating that labor force participation rose within most of the marital status and educational attainment groups. Note that all of the coefficients for the largest marital status group—married people who live with a spouse—are positive and statistically significant. Among women, the percentage-point increases in participation rates are typically larger among those with higher educational attainment. It is much harder to see this pattern among men. Only in the oldest age group, 70–74-year-olds, is there a tendency for better educated males to see a bigger jump in participation rates.

The coefficient estimates in table 1-2 can be combined with estimates of population change and the main effects of marital status and educational attainment to decompose the total change in participation rates between the portion caused by changing population composition and the part caused by higher participation rates within marital status and educational attainment groups. There are two ways to perform the decomposition, but both yield similar results. For men between 62 and 64, slightly more than half the increase in participation between 1985–91 and 2004–10 can be attributed to shifts in the composition of the 62-to-64-year-old population. More of the male population is in well-educated groups that had relatively high participation rates in 1985–91; less of it is in groups with less education and lower expected participation rates. Conversely, about 45 percent of the jump in the 62–64-year-old male participation rate was due to increasing participation rates *within* many subgroups in this population. In the two older male populations, only about one-third of the jump in overall participation was due to shifts in population composition. The remaining two-thirds of the increase was due to the rise in participation rates within many subpopulations in the age group (see table 1-2).

Among women, the change in overall participation rates was mainly due to increases in participation rates within subpopulations. Comparatively less was due to shifts in the composition of the older female population toward subgroups with high participation rates. Among women between 62 and 64, just one-third of the rise in participation can be traced to compositional shifts in the 62–64-year-old population. The remaining two-thirds was due to increases in participation rates in a number of subgroups, especially subpopulations with more-than-average schooling. In the two older women's groups, the balance of effects was even more one-sided. Between 80 and 85 percent of the jump in participation was due to increases in participation within subgroups. Only 15 to 20 percent of the rise was caused by shifts in the composition of the older female population toward groups that initially had above-average participation rates.

Table 1-2. *Regression Estimates of the Change in Labor Force Participation Rates between 1985–91 and 2004–10, by Gender, Educational Attainment, and Marital Status*

Age group and marital status	Women				Men			
	Less than high school	High school graduate	Some college	At least 4 years college	Less than high school	High school graduate	Some college	At least 4 years college
	Age 62 to 64				*Age 62 to 64*			
Married—spouse present	4.5***	12.6***	12.0***	13.8***	4.9***	3.8***	3.2***	4.4***
(Standard error)	*0.5*	*0.4*	*0.5*	*0.4*	*0.5*	*0.4*	*0.5*	*0.4*
Married—spouse absent or separated	-0.5	-4.9**	0.5	6.8***	4.3**	-0.6	-2.9	-0.9
(Standard error)	*1.7*	*2.3*	*3.4*	*2.5*	*1.7*	*2.3*	*3.4*	*2.5*
Widowed or divorced	1.5	3.6***	8.1***	4.4***	-2.6***	-0.2	2.9**	2.5**
(Standard error)	*0.9*	*0.9*	*1.2*	*1.2*	*0.9*	*0.9*	*1.2*	*1.2*
Single	1.2	1.3	-2.8	1.0	-0.7	0.7	4.5**	-4.4***
(Standard error)	*1.4*	*1.5*	*2.1*	*1.6*	*1.4*	*1.5*	*2.1*	*1.6*
	Age 65 to 69				*Age 65 to 69*			
Married—spouse present	4.0***	8.4***	10.6***	11.4***	6.2***	5.9***	5.6***	5.1***
(Standard error)	*0.3*	*0.3*	*0.4*	*0.3*	*0.3*	*0.3*	*0.4*	*0.3*
Married—spouse absent or separated	3.4**	5.8***	9.8***	6.8***	9.0***	1.2	0.7	16.3***
(Standard error)	*1.4*	*1.8*	*2.6*	*2.3*	*1.4*	*1.8*	*2.6*	*2.3*
Widowed or divorced	1.6**	8.1***	9.3***	10.9***	3.3***	5.3***	5.6***	8.5***
(Standard error)	*0.6*	*0.7*	*0.9*	*1.0*	*0.6*	*0.7*	*0.9*	*1.0*
Single	-0.1	8.2***	7.0***	9.4***	1.4	8.5***	10.8***	2.2
(Standard error)	*1.1*	*1.2*	*1.9*	*1.4*	*1.1*	*1.2*	*1.9*	*1.4*

	Age 70 to 74					Age 70 to 74		
Married—spouse present	4.5***	6.2***	5.6***	8.9***	3.3***	5.7***	3.9***	6.3***
(Standard error)	*0.3*	*0.3*	*0.4*	*0.4*	*0.3*	*0.3*	*0.4*	*0.4*
Married—spouse absent or separated	0.5	8.2***	-8.6***	9.3***	4.0***	0.2	-9.3***	-6.7**
(Standard error)	*1.3*	*1.9*	*2.5*	*2.6*	*1.3*	*1.9*	*2.5*	*2.6*
Widowed or divorced	1.5***	5.9***	5.5***	7.4***	3.3***	3.4***	3.1***	5.1***
(Standard error)	*0.5*	*0.6*	*0.9*	*0.9*	*0.5*	*0.6*	*0.9*	*0.9*
Single	2.7**	7.0***	10.3***	1.3	5.4***	5.7***	-0.7	-7.6***
(Standard error)	*1.1*	*1.2*	*2.0*	*1.6*	*1.1*	*1.2*	*2.0*	*1.6*

Source: Author's estimates with monthly CPS files for 1985–91 and 2004–10 as explained in text.

Note: In addition to the variables shown, the regression equation includes controls for seasonal adjustment, the prime-age unemployment rate, and respondents' race and exact reported year of age.

* = significant at 10 percent level; ** = significant at 5 percent level; and *** = significant at 1 percent level using two-tailed test.

In sum, workers who have above-average education tend to retire later than workers with less education. As the educational attainment of the aged has risen, the expected labor force participation rates of the aged have also increased. Among women we have also seen a stronger tendency toward delayed retirement among those who have higher levels of schooling. This tendency seems much weaker among men, where increases in labor force participation over the past two decades have been more similar across educational groups. Nonetheless, the increased level of schooling among older men has tended to boost participation rates and the relative earnings of aged workers compared with the prime-age workforce.

How Is the Delay in Retirement Divided between Part-Time and Full-Time Work?

Many older workers are employed in jobs with less-than-full-time work schedules. Most Americans past age 62 qualify for Social Security retired worker benefits, so it is less necessary for them to work long hours or on a full-time schedule to obtain an adequate income. The top panel in figure 1-5 shows the proportion of employed men and women who worked part-time schedules between 1985 and 1991, years when the trend toward early retirement reached its peak. It is plain that part-time work is more common among women than among men and far more common as workers of both sexes grow older. The fraction of working men on part-time schedules increases by a factor of six between ages 55–59 and 65–69.

Did the trend toward later retirement increase the percentage of older workers who are employed part time? A comparison of the top and bottom panels of figure 1-5 sheds light on this question. In the two oldest age groups, 65–69 and 70–74, the proportion of workers on part-time schedules edged down. In the other three age groups, the percentage of workers with part-time schedules increased, though the change among workers between 62 and 64 was not large. Thus for most of the older age groups that experienced an increase in labor force participation rates, the rise in employment left the proportion of part-time and full-time workers roughly unchanged.

Another perspective on the issue is provided in table 1-1, which shows the change in the fractions of the population in older age groups employed in full-time and part-time jobs. Note that the sum of the changes in full-time and part-time employment is equal to the total increase in the employment-population ratio for an age group. Table 1-1 shows that both full-time and part-time employment rates increased between 1985–91 and 2004–12. This was true for both sexes and for every age group between 62 and 74. Contrary to a widespread impression, the delay in retirement has involved an increase in the proportion of older people who work on both full-time and part-time schedules. At ages past 65, the increase

Figure 1-5. *Proportion of Workers on Part-Time Schedules,*
by Gender and Age, 1985–91 and 2004–10

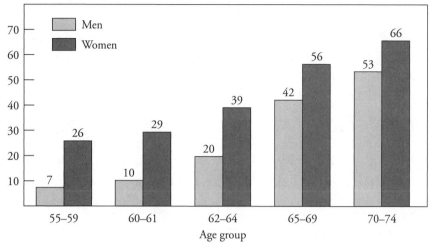

1985–91

Percent of employed persons

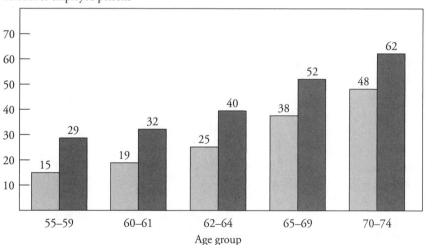

2004–10

Percent of employed persons

Source: Author's tabulations of monthly Current Population Survey files for 1985–91 and 2004–10.

in full-time work has been proportionately somewhat greater than the increase in part-time employment.

Is Later Retirement Caused by a Rise in "Bridge Jobs" or by Lengthening Career Jobs?

Workers do not need to reduce their weekly hours to reduce the demands of employment. They may also choose to work in jobs that are less stressful or that require less effort than the jobs they held during most of their careers. Such jobs are often referred to as "bridge jobs," signaling the fact that they represent a bridge between full-time work in a career job and full retirement.[8] Of course, some bridge jobs may be part time, but others may simply be less demanding or stressful than the worker's career job. In this section, I examine evidence of older workers' retention of jobs they held well before the typical retirement age. Very few of these jobs can be classified as bridge jobs.

The BLS has obtained consistent survey information about workers' job tenure in interview supplements to the standard CPS questionnaire (table 1-3). Since 1987 male job tenures have fallen at most ages while the median tenure of female workers has risen modestly except in the two oldest age categories, where it has also declined. Given the trend in women's job market experience, it is not surprising that men's and women's job tenure patterns look more similar in recent years than was the case two decades ago. Women are now more likely to remain steadily in the workforce than they were before the mid-1980s. It is surprising that male and female tenure patterns have converged mainly because average male tenure has declined rather than because female tenure has increased. Between 1987 and 2006 the median tenure of wage-earning men between the ages of 45 and 54 fell 3.7 years (31 percent), and the median tenure of men between the ages of 55 and 64 fell 5 years (34 percent).

Workers' average tenure in jobs depends on their willingness to remain in the job as well as employers' job separation policies. If workers' desire to hold on to jobs has remained roughly unchanged, the fall in average job tenure reflects an increased willingness or need on the part of employers to discharge their workers before they accumulate long tenure on the job. The evidence in table 1-3 is consistent with the view that permanent job separation is now more common for long-tenure workers than it was before the 1987 tenure survey.

The crucial issue when considering job retention among older workers, however, is not the trend in median tenures of middle-aged and older workers, but rather changes in job retention rates among older workers who already have

8. Ruhm (1990). Cahill, Giandrea, and Quinn (2006).

Table 1-3. *Median Years of Tenure with Current Employer for Employed Wage and Salary Workers by Age and Sex, Selected Years, 1987–2006*

Age in years by sex	January 1987	January 1991	February 1996	February 2000	January 2006
Both sexes					
16 and over	3.4	3.6	3.8	3.5	4.0
25 and over	5.0	4.8	5.0	4.7	4.9
Men					
16 and over	4.0	4.1	4.0	3.8	4.1
25 and over	5.7	5.4	5.3	4.9	5.0
25 to 34	3.1	3.1	3.0	2.7	2.9
35 to 44	7.0	6.5	6.1	5.3	5.1
45 to 54	11.8	11.2	10.1	9.5	8.1
55 to 64	14.5	13.4	10.5	10.2	9.5
Women					
16 and over	3.0	3.2	3.5	3.3	3.9
25 and over	4.3	4.3	4.7	4.4	4.8
25 to 34	2.6	2.7	2.7	2.5	2.8
35 to 44	4.4	4.5	4.8	4.3	4.6
45 to 54	6.8	6.7	7.0	7.3	6.7
55 to 64	9.7	9.9	10.0	9.9	9.2

Sources: U.S. Bureau of Labor Statistics. 1997. "Employee Tenure in the Mid-1990s," news release, USDL 97-25, U.S. Department of Labor (www.bls.gov/news.release/history/tenure_013097.txt); U.S. Bureau of Labor Statistics. 2006. "Employee Tenure in 2006," news release, USDL 06-1563 (www.bls.gov/news.release/archives/tenure_09082006.pdf).

lengthy tenures in their current jobs. For a 60-year-old worker who holds a career job, what is the likelihood he or she will still hold the same job three or five years later? If the probability of job retention falls, it may mean the worker has either retired or has switched to another job (possibly a bridge job). If the probability of job retention increases, there is a clear implication that at least part of the rise in old-age employment rates is traceable to an increase in the duration of career jobs.

To shed light on the issue, I assembled individual-level data on job tenure for aged and near-aged workers collected in special supplements to the monthly CPS files covering the periods 1987–91 and 2004–10. The BLS collected these data in surveys conducted in 1987, 1991, 2004, 2006, 2008, and 2010. Wage and salary and self-employed workers were asked how long they had continuously worked for their current employers. The CPS job-tenure responses were not obtained in a longitudinal survey. Thus in order to draw conclusions about job retention within a given birth cohort, it was necessary to treat the data with methods appropriate to repeated cross sections. For this purpose I derived information about the distribution of job tenures among two age groups in the 1987, 2004, and 2006 surveys: workers aged 58 to 63 and workers aged 64 to 69 at the time of the survey. I then derived data on workers in the same birth cohorts from surveys conducted four years after those three surveys, that is, in 1991, 2008, and 2010. In other words, I compiled job tenure distribution data for workers who were 62 to 67 years old or 68 to 73 years old in the 1991, 2008, and 2010 surveys.

The results of the tabulations are in table 1-4. Statistics in the top panel show tenure distributions among women; statistics in the bottom panel refer to men. The three columns on the left pertain to the younger birth cohorts (workers who were 58 to 63 in the first interview), while the three right-hand columns contain information on tenures and job retention in the older birth cohorts (workers who were between 64 and 69 at the time of the initial interview). Entries in the table show the sample sizes of CPS respondents in the indicated age and gender groups and CPS surveys. Note that the number of respondents declines in the second survey. The loss in sample size is hardly surprising, since mortality will reduce the number of surviving respondents in an aged population. I also show the weighted percentage of respondents who reported their job tenure in each survey. People who are not employed cannot report a job tenure, and some job holders did not give valid responses to the tenure question. Except among men aged 58 to 63, the job tenure question was answered by a larger proportion of the population in the most recent surveys compared with the ones conducted in 1987 and 1991. This seems plausible since, as we have seen, labor force participation and employment in older age groups has increased since 1987–91.

Other entries in table 1-4 show the weighted total number of aged workers with job tenures longer than ten or twenty years (in the case of the initial interview) or longer than fourteen or twenty-four years (in the case of the second interview). Because the first and second interviews were conducted four years apart, I can draw inferences about the proportion of job holders in the first interview who retained the same jobs in the second. For example, the 1987 CPS interview showed there were 1.321 million women between 58 and 63 who had worked continuously for the same employer for at least ten years. The 1991 CPS interview showed there were 0.544 million women between 62 and 67 who had worked continuously for the same employer for at least fourteen years. From these results we can infer that 41.2 percent (0.544 million divided by 1.321 million) of women who were between 58 and 63 and had ten years of job tenure in 1987 continued to work for the same employer four years later. Among women in the same age group in 1987 who had at least twenty years of job tenure in that year, 42.2 percent continued to work for the same employer four years later (that is, they had accumulated at least twenty-four years of job tenure by 1991).

The interesting result in table 1-4 is that job retention rates were higher in 2004–10 compared with 1987–91. For example, among men between 58 and 63 with at least ten years of job tenure in 1987, about 39 percent were still working for the same employer in 1991. Among men between 58 and 63 with at least ten years of job tenure in either 2004 or 2006, about 55 percent still worked for the same employer four years later. The 16-percentage-point increase in the job reten- tion rate implies that lengthening job tenures in late-career jobs played a role in boosting the labor force participation and employment rates of older men. The same pattern is seen in the job retention statistics for men between 64 and 69 and for women between ages 58 and 63 and between 64 and 69. As labor force par- ticipation rates have increased, we have seen higher job retention rates among older workers who hold long-tenure jobs. This finding does not rule out the pos- sibility that many older workers have moved into less stressful bridge jobs. On the contrary, the statistics on part-time employment in table 1-1 and figure 1-5 show that older workers continue to move toward shorter work schedules as they grow older. Nonetheless, the estimates in table 1-4 indicate that some of the increase in old-age labor supply can be traced to workers' willingness to stay in their career jobs until later in life.

Conclusions

In summary, since the late 1980s and early 1990s there has been a sizeable rise in labor force participation and employment at older ages. This trend represents a sharp turnaround of labor force trends during the previous century. Among 68-year-old men, the labor force participation rate increased by more than half between 1991 and 2010. Among 68-year-old women, the participation rate increased by about two-thirds. The proportional increase in labor force partic- ipation and employment has been smaller among men and women near age 60 and larger among workers between 64 and 72.

Even though there has been a marked increase in the labor supply contributions of older Americans, workers in their 60s and early 70s have not seen a drop in their relative wages. On the contrary, the wages of 62–74-year-olds have improved com- pared with the wages earned by prime-age workers (that is, workers between 35 and 54 years old). Some of the wage gain can be explained by the relative improve- ment in older workers' educational credentials. Compared with aged workers in the 1980s, today's older workers have educational attainment that is more similar to that of prime-age workers. In addition, older workers have seen an improvement in their relative earnings even if we compare them with prime-age workers who have the same educational credentials. One explanation may be that the workers who are delaying retirement and remaining in the workforce have above-average

Table 1-4. Estimated Job Retention among Older Workers, 1987–91 and 2004–10

	Age in initial survey year = 58 to 63			Age in initial survey year = 64 to 69		
	1987 and 1991	2004 and 2008	2006 and 2010	1987 and 1991	2004 and 2008	2006 and 2010
Women						
CPS sample size—initial survey year	4,328	4,060	4,423	4,013	3,196	3,279
Percent of population with reported job tenure	35.7	45.1	46.3	14.4	21.3	21.3
Persons with tenure of at least 10 years (thousands)	1,321	1,932	2,137	487	740	730
Persons with tenure of at least 20 years (thousands)	552	879	1,063	256	374	373
CPS sample size—second survey year	4,096	3,770	4,143	3,660	2,889	3,060
Percent of population with reported job tenure	20.1	29.8	30.8	8.8	13.0	14.1
Persons with tenure of at least 14 years (thousands)	544	1,022	1,051	192	325	441
Persons with tenure of at least 24 years (thousands)	233	504	502	91	165	195
Job retention rate after 4 years						
Among workers with initial tenure of at least 10 years (percent)	41.2	52.9	49.2	39.5	43.8	60.4
Among workers with initial tenure of at least 20 years (percent)	42.2	57.3	47.2	35.7	44.1	52.3
Men						
Sample size—initial survey year	3,792	3,729	4,189	3,308	2,913	2,947
Percent of population with reported job tenure	59.2	54.5	56.6	25.0	28.9	29.1
Persons with tenure at least 10 years (thousands)	2,300	2,230	2,723	789	904	911
Persons with tenure at least 20 years (thousands)	1,553	1,382	1,635	567	579	606
Sample size—second survey year	3,502	3,454	3,834	2,782	2,427	2,526
Percent of population with reported job tenure	30.2	38.0	38.4	14.6	21.3	21.3
Persons with tenure at least 14 years (thousands)	904	1,254	1,460	313	548	570
Persons with tenure at least 24 years (thousands)	554	736	850	231	330	391
Job retention rate after 4 years						
Among workers with initial tenure of at least 10 years (percent)	39.3	56.2	53.6	39.6	60.7	62.6
Among workers with initial tenure of at least 20 years (percent)	35.7	53.3	52.0	40.7	56.9	64.5

Source: Author's tabulations of CPS special supplements on worker tenure, 1985, 1991, 2004, 2006, 2008, and 2010, as explained in text.

earnings capacity, even accounting for their educational attainment. Another is that the evolution of labor demand has boosted the payoff for having experience in the labor market. It is important to recognize that the improvement in older workers' relative earnings has occurred in the face of a considerable increase in the relative supply of older workers. Not only have older Americans increased their participation and employment rates compared with Americans in younger age groups, the entry of the baby boom generation into their retirement years has boosted the share of the potential workers who are elderly or near-elderly. Between 1985 and 2010 the number of Americans aged between 15 and 59 years increased 30 percent, while the number between 60 and 74 years increased 40 percent. Despite these trends, employers have offered well-paid jobs to an increasing share of Americans aged between 60 and 74.

Increases in employment associated with the delay in retirement have been divided between increases in part-time jobs and full-time jobs. There is no evidence, especially past age 65, that the increase in employment has been disproportionately concentrated among older workers who are employed on part-time schedules. On the contrary, gains in full-time employment have been proportionately a bit faster than gains in part-time employment. It is nonetheless the case that part-time work remains much more common among older workers than it is in the prime-age workforce. The crucial point is that gains in employment linked to the delay in retirement have not been concentrated solely or even disproportionately in part-time work.

Finally, new evidence was presented on the role of career jobs in the trend toward later retirement. BLS surveys show that median job tenures among middle-aged men have declined while job tenures among working women have increased only modestly. These developments raise questions about the importance of longer career jobs in explaining the trend toward later retirement. The surveys that permit us to measure the trend in median job tenures also allow us to examine job retention rates among older workers who have already accumulated long tenures on their jobs. The estimates in this chapter show that long-tenure older workers have seen a noticeable increase in job retention rates over the past quarter century. This evidence suggests that a sizeable part of the trend to later retirement ages can be traced to lengthening careers on the part of older workers who have held their jobs for a decade or more. The finding does not minimize the importance of part-time employment or bridge jobs in the transition from career employment to full retirement, but it does suggest that an important contributor to higher old-age employment rates is the delay in many workers' retirement from career jobs.

In the wake of the severe recession and financial market turmoil in 2008 and 2009, we sometimes hear that workers are delaying their retirement because a miserable economy has made it impossible for workers to afford to retire. Earnings losses as a result of unemployment and wealth losses flowing from risky capital markets and the drop in home values has left millions of workers unprepared for retirement. Note, however, that the trend toward later retirement has been under way for more than two decades, in good times and bad. If anything, recessions have tended to slow the rise in old-age labor force participation.[9]

This chapter is primarily descriptive. It does not offer explanations for the trends it documents. It does, however, offer a clearer picture of a phenomenon that has only recently begun to attract notice in the business press and wider public. Policymakers and reporters may be vaguely aware that the average age of retirement has been rising. Most are unaware, however, that the trend has been under way for more than two decades. To develop plausible models that can account for the trend, one must first understand its scope and character.

Appendix Table 1A-1. *Labor Force Participation Rates of Aged and Near-Aged Population, by Sex, 1950–2010*

Percent of noninstitutionalized population

	Women		Men		Both sexes	
Year	55–64	65 and older	55–64	65 and older	55–64	65 and older
1950	27.0	9.7	86.9	45.8	56.7	26.7
1955	32.5	10.6	88.0	39.6	59.5	24.1
1960	37.1	10.8	86.8	33.1	60.9	20.8
1965	41.1	10.0	84.6	27.9	61.9	17.8
1970	43.0	9.7	82.9	26.8	61.8	16.9
1975	40.9	8.2	75.6	21.6	57.2	13.7
1980	41.3	8.1	72.1	19.0	55.7	12.5
1985	42.0	7.3	68.0	15.8	54.2	10.8
1990	45.2	8.6	67.8	16.3	55.9	11.8
1995	49.2	8.8	66.0	16.8	57.2	12.2
2000	51.9	9.4	67.3	17.7	59.3	12.9
2005	57.0	11.5	69.3	19.8	62.9	15.0
2010	60.2	13.7	70.0	22.1	64.9	17.3

Source: U.S. Bureau of Labor Statistics

9. Bosworth and Burtless (2011).

References

Anderson, Patricia M., Alan L. Gustman, and Thomas L. Steinmeier. 1999. "Trends in Male Labor Force Participation and Retirement: Some Evidence on the Role of Pensions and Social Security in the 1970s and 1980s." *Journal of Labor Economics* 17, no. 4: 757–83.

Bosworth, Barry P., and Gary Burtless. 2011. "Recessions, Wealth Destruction, and the Timing of Retirement." Working Paper 2010-22. Chestnut Hill, Mass.: Center for Retirement Research at Boston College.

Burtless, Gary, and Joseph F. Quinn. 2001. "Retirement Trends and Policies to Encourage Work among Older Americans." In *Ensuring Health and Income Security for an Aging Workforce,* edited by Peter Budetti and others. Kalamazoo, Mich.: W.E. Upjohn Institute for Employment Research.

———. 2002. "Is Working Longer the Answer for an Aging Workforce?" Issue in Brief 11. Chestnut Hill, Mass.: Center for Retirement Research at Boston College.

Cahill, K., M. Giandrea, and J. Quinn, 2006, "Retirement Patterns from Career Employment." *The Gerontologist* 46, no. 4: 514–23.

Ransom, Roger L., Richard Sutch, and Samuel H. Williamson. 1991. "Retirement: Past and Present." In *Retirement and Public Policy,* edited by Alicia H. Munnell. Dubuque, Iowa: Kendall Hunt.

Ruhm, Christopher J. 1990. "Bridge Jobs and Partial Retirement." *Journal of Labor Economics* 8, no. 4: 482–501.

Schmitt, John. 2003. "Creating a Consistent Hourly Wage Series from the Current Population Survey's Outgoing Rotation Group, 1979–2002." Working paper. Washington, D.C.: Center for Economic and Policy Research.

U.S. Department of Commerce, Bureau of the Census. 1975. *Historical Statistics of the United States: Colonial Times to 1970.* Washington, D.C.: Government Printing Office.

2

Future Labor Force Participation among the Aged: Forecasts from the Social Security Administration and the Author

GARY BURTLESS

The labor force participation rates of Americans past age 60 have been increasing since the mid-1980s among women and since the early 1990s among men. The Social Security Administration (SSA) expects these trends to continue, although at a slower pace, over the next three decades. Each year the Social Security Administration Board of Trustees publishes an annual report to Congress on the financial status of the federal Old-Age, Survivors, and Disability Insurance (OASDI) Trust Funds. To assess the actuarial status of the trust funds, the SSA must develop estimates of future Social Security revenues and outlays. This assessment requires the agency to forecast future employment, Social Security–taxable earnings, and expected benefit payments to pensioners. A crucial ingredient of the forecast is a prediction of future labor force participation and employment rates of men and women of different ages.

As the baseline forecast for our study, we used the SSA predictions in the intermediate (or "alternative II") projection of "The 2011 Annual Report of the Board of Trustees of the Federal Old-Age and Survivors Insurance and Federal Disability Insurance Trust Funds" (the 2011 OASDI Trustees' report). Since a principal goal of our study was to examine the impact of higher average retirement ages on the federal budget and households' financial well-being, we also developed an alternative forecast of old-age labor force participation rates (LFPRs). In particu-

The participants in the project to develop alternative forecasts, including Henry Aaron, Karen Smith and Richard Johnson of the Urban Institute, Moody's researchers, and myself, agreed on how to develop the forecasts. I developed the detailed alternative forecasts and shared my preliminary findings with the others, who found them acceptable. Karen Smith of the Urban Institute made small modifications to improve the forecast.

lar, we created a forecast in which future participation rates would climb significantly faster than predicted by the OASDI Trustees in their 2011 report to Congress. In this chapter, we describe the SSA forecast and the development of our alternative forecast.

In developing the SSA forecast, the Office of the Chief Actuary of Social Security prepares detailed, year-by-year estimates of historical and projected participation rates and employment-population ratios by two-year age groups between ages 16 and 19, by five-year age groups between ages 20 and 69, and for the entire population age 16 and older and age 70 and older, separately for women and men. The detailed projections also include a forecast of labor force participation rates for individual ages between 55 and 79, separately for women and men. In combination with the Social Security actuary's detailed forecast of the future population by individual year of age, the estimates of labor force participation rates can be used to predict the future labor force of women and men within five-year age groups and, for the population between 55 and 79, by exact year of age. In developing our alternative forecast, we focused on the projections for the older labor force, that is, Americans who are 55 and older. We accepted without any change the SSA forecasts of future labor force participation rates among age groups younger than 55.

In 2011 the OASDI Trustees predicted that future old-age labor force participation rates would eventually increase compared with their depressed levels in 2010. However, the trustees' estimates of some old-age participation rates in 2010 were, in fact, below the participation rates later estimated by the Bureau of Labor Statistics (BLS). For men aged 55–59, for example, the 2010 participation rate predicted by the trustees was 0.7 percentage point below the actual rate estimated by the BLS; for men 60–64, the 2010 error was –0.4 percentage point; and for women 55–59, the 2010 error was –0.8 percentage point. For men older than 65 and women older than 60, the errors were smaller and in some cases positive. For the entire population past age 55 the error was –0.3 percentage point for men and –0.2 percentage point for women. Even though the 2011 Trustees' report predicted a partial recovery from the low participation rates of 2010, the recovery among 55–64-year-old men is modest. For women between 55 and 59 the SSA forecast predicted no recovery at all. During the entire forecast period between 2011 and 2045 the predicted participation rate of 55–59-year-old women remained below its average level in 2008–10.

For reasons explained later, our alternative forecast of future participation rates past age 60 depends crucially on the predicted participation rates of men and women between 55 and 59. Thus, in preparing our alternative forecast we adjusted the trustees' projection of 2011–40 participation rates for both men and women between 55 and 59 to eliminate the spurious drop that occurs in the 2011

Figure 2-1. *Male Labor Force Participation Rates in Indicated Age Groups and Trustees' Forecast, 1976–2030*

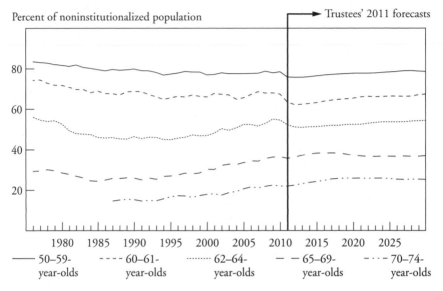

Source: U.S. Bureau of Labor Statistics and Office of Chief Actuary, U.S. Social Security Administration (2011).

OASDI Trustees' report forecast. In particular, we assume that the future participation rates of 55–59-year-olds never fall below the 2010 participation rates reported by the BLS. As will be seen, our method of forecasting participation rates for those who are 60 and older also implies that age-specific participation rates above age 60 will never fall below their observed levels in 2010.

The assumption that future participation rates will not decline below their level in 2010 implies that our 2011 alternative forecast of participation rates is above the baseline forecast in the 2011 Trustees' report. Figures 2-1 and 2-2 show the historical participation rates for 1976–2010 and the trustees' 2011 projections for 2011–30. Figure 2-1 displays the trends in participation rates for men in five older age groups—ages 55–59, 60–61, 62–64, 65–69, and 70–74. Figure 2-2 shows participation rates for women in the same five age groups. Even a cursory examination of the two charts suggests that the 2011 Trustees' report must imply a considerable slowdown in the trend toward later retirement. In nearly all age groups, the intermediate forecast implies that age-specific participation rates will climb more slowly in the two decades after 2010 than they did in the two decades between 1990 and 2010.

Figure 2-2. *Female Labor Force Participation Rates in Indicated Age Groups and Trustees' Forecast, 1976–2030*

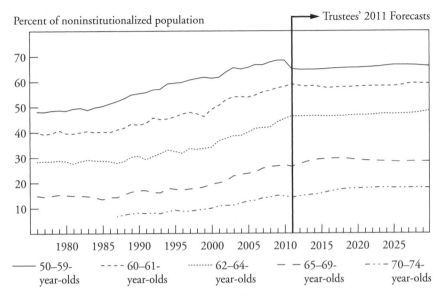

Source: U.S. Bureau of Labor Statistics and Office of Chief Actuary, U.S. Social Security Administration (2011).

To project future participation rates under the assumption of a faster trend toward later retirement, we estimated cohort labor force participation "persistence rates" at successive ages between ages 60 and 80 separately for women and men. A birth-year cohort's persistence rate at a given age is simply its labor force participation rate at that age measured as a percentage of the cohort's participation rate when the cohort was 57 years old. These estimates were obtained from BLS-supplied tabulations of monthly Current Population Survey (CPS) files for calendar years 1976–2010. The derivation of our "persistence rate" estimates is described in chapter 1. Figure 1-2 in that chapter shows how labor force persistence rates have trended over the period from 1976 through 2010. Figure 1-3 in that chapter shows how much labor force persistence increased at each age between 60 and 79. In particular, the chart shows how much persistence increased between 1988–90, when the trend toward later retirement began, and 2008–10, the most recent years of detailed labor force participation rate data when the tabulations were performed. For both women and men, the trends in persistence show a striking slowdown in workers' exit from the labor force, especially between ages 64 and 70.

Figure 2-3. *Male Labor Force Participation Rates in Indicated Age Groups and Trustees' and Author's Forecast, 1976–2030*

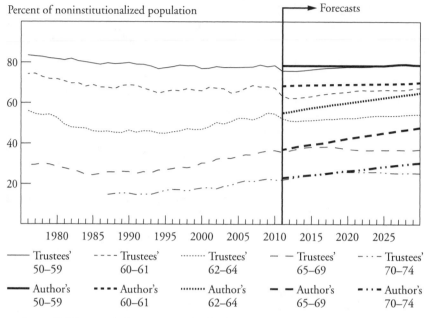

Source: U.S. Bureau of Labor Statistics and Office of Chief Actuary, U.S. Social Security Administration (2011), and author's calculations as explained in text.

In developing our forecast of future old-age participation rates, we assumed that labor force persistence will continue to increase in the future at the same rate observed between 1988–90 and 2008–10. (Before the mid-1980s, labor force participation persistence rates declined. In other words, the average age at retirement for both women and men tended to decline until the mid-1980s.) Figures 2-3 and 2-4 show predictions based on this assumption. For ages between 60 and 79 the estimates are derived by assuming:

—The future trend in participation rates among 55–59-year-olds follows the patterns displayed in the top lines in figures 2-3 and 2-4.[1]

1. In other words, we assume that the participation rates of 55–59-year-olds do not drop below their average level in 2008–10 in any year after 2010. In most years this represents an increase in the labor force participation rate compared with the projections in the 2011 Trustees' report. The only exception is in the period from 2026 through 2030 for 55–59-year-old men. For those years the 2011 Trustees' report projects a slight rise in the male participation rate compared with its average level between 2008 and 2010. In our alternative forecast of the participation rate for 55–59-year-old men, we use the Trustees' report projections if they are higher than the average participation rate between 2008 and 2010.

Figure 2-4. *Female Labor Force Participation Rates in Indicated Age Groups and Trustees' and Author's Forecast, 1976–2030*

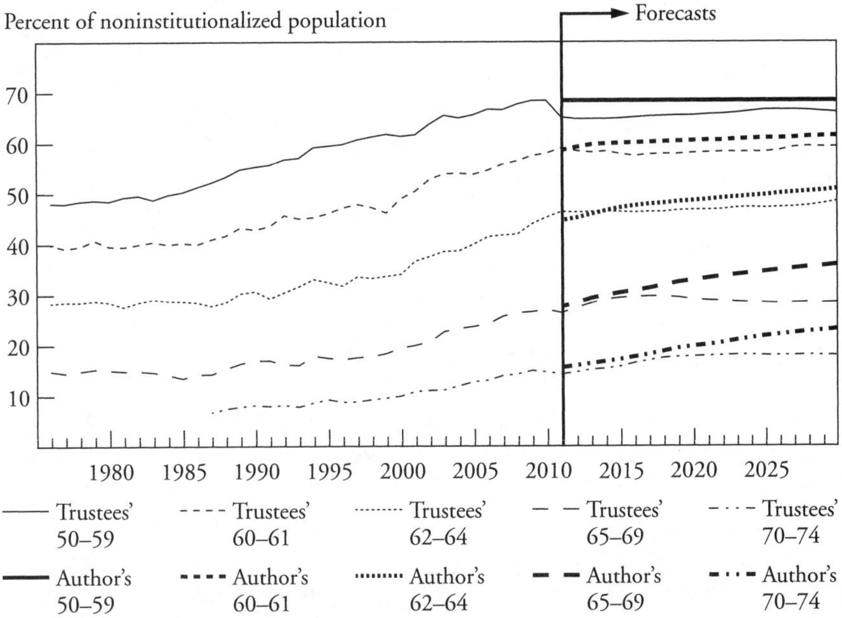

Source: U.S. Bureau of Labor Statistics and Office of Chief Actuary, U.S. Social Security Administration (2011), and author's calculations as explained in text.

—The trend increase in labor force participation persistence observed between 1988–90 and 2008–10 continues without interruption through 2040.

—If our initial forecast of the labor force participation rate at a given age and in a given year is below the participation rate predicted in the 2011 Trustees' report for that age and year, we use the 2011 Trustees' report forecast instead of our initial forecast.

—Whatever the result implied by the assumptions and the steps mentioned earlier, we require that the labor force participation persistence rate for a given cohort must be nonincreasing as the cohort grows one year older. This constraint eliminates the possibility that a given cohort will see its labor force participation rate increase between, say, ages 68 and 69 or ages 73 and 74. This constraint, however, is rarely binding and has only a minimal impact on future projected labor force participation rates.

Figures 2-3 and 2-4 show the implications of our assumptions and procedures for predicting future labor force participation rates. The lines designated "Author's" show alternative projections for the indicated age group. The other points in the charts show historical participation rates as estimated by the BLS or the 2011–30 participation rates predicted by the actuary's office in support of the Social Security Trustees' 2011 intermediate (or alternative II) assumptions.

Figure 2-5 shows the effects of our alternative participation rate forecast on the future labor supply of the population aged 55 and older. The chart compares the future labor force of older Americans under the two sets of projections. The top panel shows the total number of men past age 55 who are predicted to participate in the labor force. The lower line in that panel indicates the projections of the Social Security actuary; the upper line represents our alternative forecast in which future retirements occur at more advanced ages than are projected by the Social Security Trustees. The middle panel shows the same set of estimates for women older than 55. The bottom panel shows the percentage gap between the predicted labor force under the two alternative forecasts. Between 2011 and 2014 the alternative forecast predicts a bigger percentage increase in the male workforce than in the female labor force. This increase is mainly because the SSA Trustees' 2011 forecast predicts a noticeable drop-off in the participation rates of 55–64-year-old men between 2010 and 2011, whereas the SSA forecast predicts a sizeable decline in the female participation rates only between ages 55–59 (figures 2-1 and 2-2). Under the assumptions of our alternative forecast, the large decline in participation rates between 2010 and 2011 will not occur for either men or women. Clearly, our assumption about future participation rates will have a larger impact on men than on women. Starting in 2015 the proportional increases in male and female participation rates are comparable in size. By 2030 the predicted older female labor force is 10.6 percent higher under our alternative forecast than it is under the SSA Trustees' 2011 projection; the predicted older male labor force is 10.6 percent higher under our alternative forecast.

The future old-age labor supply is higher under the alternative forecast than it is under the trustees' 2011 projection for two reasons. First, unlike the SSA projection, our alternative forecast rests on the assumption that cohorts that retire in the future will show greater labor force participation persistence than earlier cohorts. We assume that the upward trend in persistence will approximate the upward trend seen in BLS statistics between 1988–90 and 2008–10. This means that for any given labor force participation rate before age 60, when we assume the retirement process begins, a larger percentage of the cohort's members will remain in the workforce at each successive age past age 59. Second, the actual participation rate of 55–59-year-old men and women was higher in 2010 than estimated or predicted in the SSA Trustees' 2011 projection. Unlike the trustees, we assume that the participation rate of 55–59-year-olds will not fall below its average level in 2008–10. Because all our future predictions of participation rates after age 59 are keyed to the actual or predicted participation rate of a birth cohort

Figure 2-5. *Size of Labor Force Age 55 and Older under Alternative Forecasts, 2010–30*

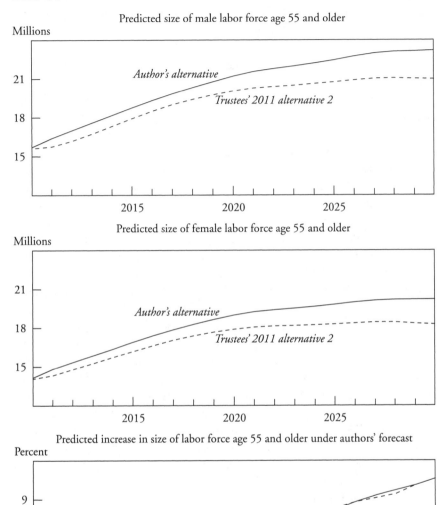

Source: U.S. Bureau of Labor Statistics, Office of Chief Actuary, U.S. Social Security Administration (2011), and author's calculations as explained in text.

when it was between 55 and 59, the upward adjustment in the 55–59 participation rate boosts future participation rates after age 59, even if we assumed that the labor force participation persistence of younger cohorts matches the persistence estimates implicit in the SSA Trustees' 2011forecast.

We can decompose the difference in the two forecasts between the two explanations just mentioned. First, we recalculated our forecast leaving unchanged the predicted future participation rates of 55–59-year-old men and women. The only difference between this modified forecast and that of the SSA Trustees is the predicted labor-force participation persistence of successive cohorts. Second, we calculated our forecast changing *both* the assumed future participation rates of 55–59-year-olds *and* the projected future persistence rates. The difference between these two forecasts gives us an estimate of the effect of increasing the 55–59 participation rates to reflect the trustees' prediction error for 2010. For men, between 67 percent and 94 percent of the difference between our labor force predictions and those of the trustees are due to our assumption that future persistence rates will continue to rise (or will rise faster on average than predicted by the trustees). The remaining 6 percent to 33 percent of the difference is explained by the fact that the trustees predict a sizeable drop in the participation rates of 55–59-year-old men after 2008–10. If that drop is eliminated, future participation rates at ages past 59 will also be higher than predicted by the SSA Trustees. By 2030, only about 6 percent of the gap between the trustees' projection and our alternative forecast is due to this factor. For women a much larger fraction of the difference in the predicted aged labor force is due to the increase in the predicted participation rate of 55–59-year-olds. This is because the proportional impact of the larger 55–59-year-old female workforce by itself represents a large part of the difference between the SSA Trustees' forecast and our alternative forecast, especially in the early years of the forecast. By 2030 this factor still accounts for about half the difference in old-age labor force predictions between the two forecasts. Thus, for women much more than for men, our alternative forecast generates a larger predicted future labor force because the assumed future participation rate of 55–59-year-olds is higher than predicted by the trustees.

It is worth emphasizing that neither the SSA Trustees' 2011 participation rate forecast nor our alternative forecast represents a prediction of *actual* future labor supply. Both sets of predictions forecast the number of Americans who will work or be seeking work in future years. Many will be unsuccessful in finding work. If the unemployment rate is high, as was the case during and after the Great Recession, a sizeable percentage of labor force participants will fail to land a job. Because our alternative forecast of future participation rates predicts there will be more participants than predicted by the SSA Trustees, a larger percentage of predicted participants is likely to be unemployed. This crucial feature of the forecast is considered at length in chapter 3.

Our alternative forecast of faster future growth in old-age labor force participation rates should not be interpreted as our best estimate of the future growth in desired labor supply among older workers. Instead, it is an alternative but plausible forecast based on recent historical experience. A goal of this volume is to show how government revenues and outlays and household financial circumstances would be affected if workers delayed their exits from the workforce. Of course, we could have developed an alternative forecast in which older Americans increase their desired labor supply even faster than they have done in the recent past. However, we believe the alternative forecast we have adopted has an attractive feature: it allows us to report revenue and outlay changes and estimates of household income gains under a set of assumptions that are easy to understand. In essence, we are simply assuming that future changes in older workers' willingness to remain in the workforce will follow trends we have observed over the two decades ending in 2010.

3

Impact of Higher Retirement Ages on Public Budgets: Simulation Results from DYNASIM3

KAREN E. SMITH AND RICHARD W. JOHNSON

The graying of America is often described as an aging crisis. Actually, it presents an enormous opportunity and is a cause for celebration. The elderly population is growing because longevity has soared. Americans are now living longer and healthier than ever before. The challenge is to harness the talents of an increasingly capable group of older citizens to support the nation's continued prosperity. This chapter examines how increased labor force participation by people over age 55 might affect household and government budgets.[1]

The long-term fiscal outlook, now rather bleak, would improve if older workers delayed retirement. Over the next fifty years, Social Security actuaries anticipate that the number of Social Security beneficiaries per 100 workers will rise from thirty-five to forty-nine.[2] By working longer than is currently assumed, older Americans could reduce the number of people drawing benefits and the budget cost of those benefits, support their current consumption from current earnings, and generate added taxes that would help cover the costs of both retirement programs and other government services. Prior research found that Americans could increase their annual consumption at older ages by more than 25 percent if they retired at age 67 instead of age 62.[3] Everyone would gain by working longer, but

1. See Smith and Johnson (2013) for a longer version of our study with more detailed tables and many additional simulation results.
2. Board of Trustees (2011).
3. Butrica and others (2004).

46

lower-income workers would gain most. Additional Social Security taxes generated by five additional years of work by nondisabled older Americans would off-set more than half of the Social Security Trust Fund deficit in 2045. Moreover, if the additional federal and state income tax revenue generated from this additional work went to Social Security, the system could remain solvent through 2045 without any benefit cuts.[4] This chapter uses the Urban Institute's Dynamic Simulation of Income Model (DYNASIM3) to estimate the impact of a continuation over the next three decades of recent trends toward delayed retirement on government budgets and household income.

The innovation in this chapter is that we use DYNASIM3 to identify those people most likely to delay retirement, given their health, demographic, and economic circumstances, while meeting externally generated labor participation targets that substantially exceed current projections by the Social Security Trustees. We also incorporate macroeconomic forecasts from Moody's Econometrics that take account of labor demand and the U.S. economy's ability to absorb these older workers. It is not a forecast of the actual course of employment, output, or government revenues and spending. Rather, we show the impact on each of those quantities should labor supply exceed projections built into official Social Security projections. We address the following questions:

—How would later retirement affect government revenues?

—How would later retirement affect government outlays, particularly on programs targeted to the aged?

—Which people are most likely to delay their retirements?

—How would later retirement change household income for different groups of workers?

—What is the impact of later retirement on government revenues and outlays for different groups of workers?

In brief, we find that continuation of the recent trend toward later retirement will increase net government revenues relative to the baseline by about 5.2 percent between 2010 and 2040 or about 0.4 percent of gross domestic product. It will also boost household net incomes of 65–69-year-olds in 2040 by 7.8 percent. High-income workers, who typically work full time for the full year, are negligibly affected by the assumed delayed retirement. The big gainers are workers in the bottom half of the income distribution. Net income of 65–69-year-olds is projected to increase 38 percent for those in the bottom income quintile and 20 percent for those in the second-lowest quintile. African Americans, Hispanics, and lower-educated seniors gain more than whites and better-educated seniors.

4. Butrica, Smith, and Steuerle (2006).

How We Did the Simulations

The projections were generated by using DYNASIM3, the Urban Institute's dynamic microsimulation model. DYNASIM3 starts with a sample of 103,072 people from the 1990 to 1993 panels of the Survey of Income and Program Participation,[5] and then ages this sample annually to 2085. The model integrates trends and group differences in life-course processes, including birth, death, schooling, leaving home, first marriage, remarriage, divorce, disability, work, retirement, and benefit take-up. It projects major sources of income and wealth from age 18 until death. DYNASIM3 projects the likelihood that people work each year based on their age, sex, race and ethnicity, education, health and disability status, geographic region, marital status, student status, number of young children, spouse characteristics (employment, age, disability, and education), immigrant status, Social Security benefit status, cohort, and state-specific unemployment rate.[6] Baseline employment, economic, and demographic variables are aligned to the 2011 Social Security Trustees' intermediate-cost projections.[7]

DYNASIM3 projects income for all household members aged 18 and older. Income sources include Social Security benefits, private pension income, earnings, and Supplemental Security Income (SSI). DYNASIM3 also projects financial assets that households accumulate as members work and save and then decumulate as members retire and spend wealth to support consumption in retirement. Using this household wealth, DYNASIM3 projects associated annual asset income including interest, dividends, and rental income, as well as taxable retirement account withdrawals and capital gains.

People are considered employed in a year if they have any earnings at all, even if they worked few hours. DYNASIM3 employment rates therefore differ from those of the Bureau of Labor Statistics (BLS), which are annual averages of monthly employment. DYNASIM3 selects people to work based on predicted employment probabilities and then selects the precise number of workers in each population group to meet specified targets, starting with those with the highest employment probabilities and proceeding to those with lower probabilities as needed.

5. Survey of Income and Program Participation (SIPP) is a household survey conducted by the United States Census Bureau to provide accurate and comprehensive information about the income and transfer program participation of American individuals and households.

6. The likelihood also includes an estimated individual-specific error term that captures nonvarying individual preferences that are independent of observed characteristics.

7. The model classifies an individual as employed if his or her expected probability of working exceeds some random number. The selection criteria are adjusted so that our baseline employment projections for men and women within particular age groups match Social Security projections.

Simulations

The DYNASIM3 baseline uses the demographic and economic assumptions from "The 2011 Annual Report of the Board of Trustees of the Federal Old-Age and Survivors Insurance and Federal Disability Insurance Trust Funds," published by the Social Security Administration and known as the 2011 Trustees' report. We contrast this baseline with three alternative scenarios, each of which increases the labor force participation of older workers.

In alternative 1, we replace the baseline employment targets with the projections described in chapter 2. Those projections gradually raise the labor supply of older workers aged 55 to 79 compared with the baseline, beginning in 2010. As with the baseline scenario, we selected individuals to work based on their ranked employment participation probabilities. All of the workers selected to work in the baseline, together with all older workers who want to work, using the higher employment targets, find employment in alternative 1.

Other projection scenarios recognize that boosting older adults' labor supply might raise unemployment. Using DYNASIM3's baseline and alternative 1 projections, Moody's Analytics (MA) generated macroeconomic forecasts that consider whether the economy can absorb all older adults who want to work. It projects that the current weakness in the labor market would slow the absorption of additional older workers until about 2018, when the U.S. economy is assumed to return to full employment. Before 2019, the increased labor supply by older adults will raise unemployment.

In alternative 2, we assume that only the newly added, older workers are excluded from work when labor demand is insufficient to maintain full employment. After 2018, when full employment is assumed to return, we assume all new workers find jobs as simulated in the unadjusted alternative simulation (see figure 3-1).

In alternative 3, we assume that the bulk of the new older workforce represents current workers who delay retirement and are unaffected by the lack of labor demand. Instead, we reduce the annual hours worked for underemployed workers to reflect longer periods of unemployment. Underemployed individuals are those projected to work fewer than 1,000 hours in the calendar year or who were unemployed for the entire preceding calendar year. We calculate reduction factors for hours worked so that the aggregate annual earnings loss equals the gap in aggregate earnings between the constrained and unconstrained simulations. In alternative 3, all underemployed workers work fewer annual hours than in alternative 1, regardless of age. Fully employed older workers work at levels simulated in alternative 1.

Figure 3-1. *Percent Change in Employment by Year and Simulation*

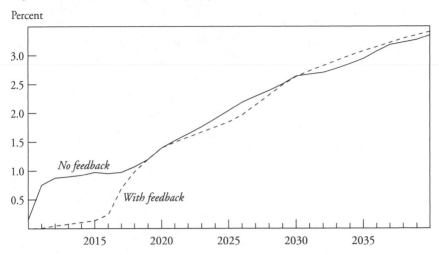

Source: The Urban Institute DYNASIM3 projections with macroeconomic feedback effects estimated by Moody's Analytics.

Simulation Results

Table 3-1 shows changes from baseline in employment, hours, and earnings under each of the three scenarios starting in 2010. As noted earlier, the baseline employment rates are aligned to labor force participation rates from the 2011 Trustees' report. By assumption, differences between alternative 1 and baseline employment rates are initially small, but grow over time. Increases in aggregate employment start small and grow gradually to more than 3 percentage points at the end of the projection period. In alternatives 2 and 3, the gains are delayed until 2019, as the continuing effects of the recession prevent some workers from finding jobs. Employment gains are greater for the 65–69-year-old group than for any other age group, growing over time to 14.7 percentage points in 2040 (see figure 3-2). In alternative 1, we assume no changes in underlying employment among people aged 15 through 54 and 80 and older. Employment rates are identical across all three alternative simulations after 2018, when we project the economy will have returned to full employment.

The percentage increase in the number of hours worked is somewhat smaller than the increase in employment, because DYNASIM3 projects that many labor force entrants will work less than full time. The percentage increase in earnings is smaller still because the earnings of those whose retirements are delayed average less than earnings of workers who are assumed to be in the labor force in the

Table 3-1. *Percent Change in Aggregate Number of Workers, Hours Worked, and Earnings Compared with the Baseline for Selected Years by Simulation*

Percent

Year	Number of workers[a]			Hours worked			Earnings[b]		
	Alt1	Alt2	Alt3	Alt1	Alt2	Alt3	Alt1	Alt2	Alt3
2010	0.16	0.00	0.16	0.16	0.00	−0.08	0.16	0.00	−0.01
2015	0.94	0.17	0.94	0.87	0.17	−0.06	0.77	0.15	0.08
2020	1.35	1.35	1.35	1.19	1.19	1.19	0.91	0.91	0.91
2025	1.98	1.98	1.98	1.67	1.67	1.67	1.25	1.25	1.25
2030	2.57	2.57	2.57	2.18	2.18	2.18	1.59	1.59	1.59
2035	2.88	2.88	2.88	2.45	2.45	2.45	1.73	1.73	1.73
2040	3.26	3.26	3.26	2.72	2.72	2.72	1.94	1.94	1.94

Source: Authors' tabulations from DYNASIM3.

a. Workers are individuals with any earnings in the calendar year.

b. Earnings include covered and uncovered earnings in wage and salary and self-employment jobs.

baseline. The reasoning is simple: comparatively high earnings is one of the major factors that cause people to defer retirement. For that reason, economywide average earnings fall slightly when retirement is delayed (see table 3-2).

Because delayed retirement increases aggregate earnings, both payroll and income tax revenues rise (table 3-3). The thirty-year cumulative increase in payroll

Figure 3-2. *Employment Rate by Age and Simulation, 2040*

Percent

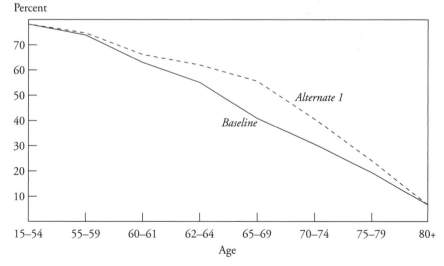

Source: Authors' tabulations from DYNASIM3.

Table 3-2. *Percent Change in Average Earnings of Workers Compared to the Baseline for Selected Years by Simulation*

Percent

	Simulation		
Year	Alt1	Alt2	Alt3
2010	0.00	0.00	−0.16
2015	−0.17	−0.02	−0.85
2020	−0.43	−0.43	−0.43
2025	−0.71	−0.71	−0.71
2030	−0.96	−0.96	−0.96
2035	−1.12	−1.12	−1.12
2040	−1.28	−1.28	−1.28

Source: Authors' tabulations from DYNASIM3.

taxes will reach $659 billion for alternative 1 (1.05 percent more than the baseline), $624 billion for alternative 2 (0.99 percent more than baseline), and $614 billion for alternative 3 (0.98 percent more than baseline). These totals include all Social Security and Medicare payroll taxes, including the increased tax on unearned income imposed by the Affordable Care Act, starting in 2013.

Delayed retirement boosts income taxes more than payroll taxes. Simulated federal income taxes are affected by changes in savings, pensions, and Social Security in the long run, affecting income tax collections well into the future. In 2040 DYNASIM3 projects that total federal income taxes will increase 1.93 percent for a thirty-year cumulative increase of $1.54 trillion for alternative 1 (1.38 percent more than baseline), $1.46 trillion for alternative 2 (1.31 percent more than baseline), and $1.46 trillion for alternative 3 (1.31 percent more than baseline). The increase in payroll taxes is identical across the three alternative simulations once the economy returns to full employment. Delayed retirement also boosts Medicare premiums by raising incomes, reducing the number of beneficiaries qualifying for subsidies, and increasing the number paying more than the standard premium.

The projected drop in average earnings per worker has important consequences for Social Security, because various Social Security provisions are indexed to changes in average earnings of covered workers. These provisions include the earnings required to receive credit for a quarter of coverage, the Social Security taxable maximum, the wage index factors used to calculate average indexed monthly earnings, the bend points used in the primary insurance amount, and ultimately the benefits paid. A reduction in the growth of the wage index also lowers the share of earnings of highly compensated workers that are taxable. A

Table 3-3. *Cumulative Dollar and Percent Change in Payroll Tax, Federal Income Tax, and Medicare Premiums Compared with the Baseline for Selected Years by Simulation*

Percent, unless otherwise noted

Year	Payroll tax[a]			Federal income tax[b]			Medicare premiums[c]		
	Alt1	Alt2	Alt3	Alt1	Alt2	Alt3	Alt1	Alt2	Alt3
2010	0.12	0.00	−0.05	0.18	0.00	−0.06	0.02	0.00	0.05
2015	0.61	0.12	−0.07	0.58	0.12	−0.26	0.08	−0.01	0.11
2020	0.71	0.71	0.71	0.75	0.77	0.72	0.16	0.15	0.09
2025	0.99	0.98	0.99	1.23	1.16	1.22	0.33	0.26	0.28
2030	1.16	1.16	1.16	1.43	1.40	1.44	0.42	0.36	0.38
2035	1.27	1.27	1.27	1.69	1.67	1.68	0.82	0.77	0.75
2040	1.38	1.38	1.38	1.93	1.91	1.93	0.70	0.67	0.69
Cumulative change 2010 to 2040									
Percent	1.05	0.99	0.98	1.38	1.31	1.31	0.54	0.49	0.49
$Billions	$659	$624	$614	$1,537	$1,465	$1,456	$36	$33	$33

Source: Authors' tabulations from DYNASIM3.

a. Payroll taxes include Social Security's Old-Age, Survivors, and Disability Insurance (OASDI) and Medicare's Hospital Insurance (HI) taxes and the Medicare Hospital Insurance surtax on unearned income beginning in 2013.

b. Federal income tax includes tax on Social Security benefits assuming 2012 current law tax policy.

c. Medicare premiums include part B and part D income adjusted premiums paid by beneficiaries less subsidies for low-income beneficiaries.

reduction in the average wage index lowers Social Security benefits per person for all new beneficiaries, even those whose simulated work effort is unchanged relative to the baseline (see table 3-4).

Aggregate Social Security benefits paid initially decline both because of the wage effect on the benefit formula and because workers who delay retirement also delay claiming their benefits, reducing the number of beneficiaries in the short term. But benefits increase in later years as newly simulated workers eventually claim and receive higher benefits.[8] By 2040 projected annual Social Security costs decline by $117 billion for alternative 1 (−0.21 percent of cumulative baseline costs), $145 billion for alternative 2 (−0.25 percent of cumulative baseline costs), and $202 billion for alternative 3 (−0.36 percent of cumulative baseline costs).

In addition to simulating earnings, DYNASIM3 also indicates how earnings affect savings, pension benefits, Social Security, and SSI benefits, all of which influence the timing of when workers claim Social Security, as well as their access

8. Social Security benefits increase both because of higher lifetime earnings and lower actuarial reductions from delayed claiming.

Table 3-4. *Cumulative Dollar and Percent Change in Aggregate Social Security Benefits Paid, Medicare Cost, and SSI Compared with the Baseline for Selected Years by Simulation*

Percent, unless otherwise noted

Year	Social Security benefits paid[a]			Medicare cost			Supplemental Security Income (SSI)		
	Alt1	*Alt2*	*Alt3*	*Alt1*	*Alt2*	*Alt3*	*Alt1*	*Alt2*	*Alt3*
2010	−0.08	0.00	−0.04	−0.06	0.00	−0.03	0.02	0.00	0.16
2015	−0.27	−0.05	−0.29	−0.20	−0.04	−0.13	−0.52	−0.09	0.34
2020	−0.33	−0.47	−0.62	−0.50	−0.50	−0.50	−0.37	−0.40	−0.08
2025	−0.27	−0.38	−0.51	−0.85	−0.85	−0.85	−0.29	−0.29	−0.13
2030	−0.37	−0.46	−0.55	−1.04	−1.04	−1.04	−0.78	−0.70	−0.44
2035	−0.15	−0.21	−0.28	−1.10	−1.10	−1.10	−0.88	−0.81	−0.52
2040	0.10	0.06	0.01	−1.32	−1.32	−1.32	−1.08	−1.03	−0.76
Cumulative change 2010 to 2040									
Percent	−0.21	−0.25	−0.36	−0.93	−0.91	−0.92	−0.62	−0.54	−0.24
$Billions	−$117	−$145	−$202	−$420	−$413	−$417	−$8	−$7	−$3

Source: Authors' tabulations from DYNASIM3.

a. Social Security benefits include Old-Age, Survivors, and Disability Insurance benefits and Social Security benefits paid to children.

to employer-provided health insurance, which in turn affects how much is spent on Medicare.

Increased labor force participation among older workers reduces Medicare spending. By 2040, projected annual Medicare costs decline by 1.32 percent. Cumulative Medicare savings over thirty years are $420 billion for alternative 1 (−0.93 percent of cumulative baseline costs), $413 billion savings for alternative 2 (−0.91 percent of cumulative baseline costs), and $417 billion savings for alternative 3 (−0.92 percent of cumulative baseline costs). Medicare savings eventually exceed Social Security savings partly because we assume that all seniors, regardless of employment status, claim Social Security by age 70, when the delayed retirement credit ends, whereas some workers wait until after age 70 to enroll in Medicare parts B and D.[9]

We show the total impact on all government spending, all government revenues, and the combined effect on the government budget in table 3-5. The change in net government revenue is the sum of changes in federal income taxes, payroll taxes, and Medicare premiums (net of the cost of the Medicare Saving

9. Individuals can work and collect Social Security benefits, though benefits are reduced before the full retirement age, currently 66, for high-earning workers.

Table 3-5. *Percent Change in Aggregate Revenues, Outlays, and Net Government Spending Compared with the Baseline for Selected Years by Simulation*
Percent, unless otherwise noted

	Revenue[a]			Outlays[b]			Net spending[c]		
Year	Alt1	Alt2	Alt3	Alt1	Alt2	Alt3	Alt1	Alt2	Alt3
2010	0.14	0.00	−0.05	−0.07	0.00	−0.03	0.65	0.00	−0.08
2015	0.58	0.12	−0.17	−0.34	−0.05	−0.21	1.62	0.31	−0.14
2020	0.71	0.72	0.69	−0.72	−0.63	−0.67	2.43	2.34	2.33
2025	1.11	1.06	1.10	−1.25	−1.12	−1.17	4.36	4.09	4.24
2030	1.30	1.28	1.30	−2.08	−1.93	−1.97	5.97	5.70	5.83
2035	1.52	1.50	1.51	−2.73	−2.57	−2.61	7.21	6.94	7.02
2040	1.71	1.70	1.71	−3.57	−3.38	−3.43	8.33	8.06	8.15
Cumulative change 2010 to 2040									
Percent	1.23	1.17	1.16	−2.02	−1.87	−1.92	5.55	5.20	5.24
$Billions	$2,232	$2,121	$2,103	−$2,089	−$1,925	−$1,979	$4,321	$4,046	$4,082

Source: Authors' tabulations from DYNASIM3.

a. Revenue includes federal income taxes, payroll taxes, and Medicare premiums.

b. Outlays include Social Security, SSI, Medicare cost, and Medicare subsidies less interest savings from lower deficits.

c. Net spending is revenue minus outlays.

Program and subsidies paid to low-income enrollees in Medicare part D). The change in government spending is the sum of the change in spending on Medicare, Social Security, and SSI, less the interest savings from lower government debt. The budget impact is the change in revenues minus the change in spending. The reduction in debt by 2040 totals $4 trillion, or about 0.4 percent of cumulative projected gross domestic product between 2010 and 2040.

Table 3-6 shows the change under alternative 1 in the number of workers with positive earnings and beneficiaries of various government programs. Increased labor force participation among older workers lowers the number of Old-Age and Survivor Insurance (OASI) Social Security beneficiaries but has virtually no impact on the number of Social Security Disability Insurance beneficiaries. As workers delay claiming retirement benefits, they also reduce the number of dependent-child Social Security beneficiaries. The number of Medicare hospital insurance enrollees increases because more workers gain Medicare entitlement by adding covered work years to their lifetime earnings and become eligible for coverage at age 65. More important, however, is a decline in the number enrolled in Medicare parts B and D because some older workers receive health insurance from their employers and delay Medicare supplemental insurance enrollment.

Table 3-6. *Change in Number of Workers, Social Security Beneficiaries,*
Medicare Enrollees, and SSI Beneficiaries Compared with the Baseline
for Alternate 1 by Year[a]

Thousands

	Change (Alternative 1 - Baseline)						
	Year						
	2010	*2015*	*2020*	*2025*	*2030*	*2035*	*2040*
Workers	263	1,669	2,497	3,736	4,970	5,707	6,630
Social Security DI beneficiaries	0	0	0	0	0	0	0
Social Security OASI beneficiaries	−20	−131	−264	−344	−432	−427	−439
Social Security children beneficiaries	0	−8	−9	−15	−20	−38	−26
Medicare HI Enrollees	0	0	0	3	5	10	10
Medicare part B enrollees	−12	−52	−162	−300	−404	−357	−502
Medicare part D enrollees	−8	−40	−141	−240	−324	−281	−427
SSI beneficiaries	3	−27	−25	−22	−68	−47	−70
Part B Medicare savings program	−11	−80	−166	−242	−365	−432	−483
Part D low-income subsidy	−10	−78	−168	−241	−377	−392	−495

Source: Authors' tabulations from DYNASIM3.

a. Table includes all individuals. Supplemental Security Income (SSI) enrollment includes federal adult SSI beneficiaries only. DI = Disability Insurance, OASI = Old-Age and Survivors Insurance, HI = Medicare Hospital Insurance.

The increase in work and earnings in alternatives 1, 2, and 3 boosts per capita income before taxes and transfers. It also changes taxes and transfers and net per capita income (table 3-7). In general, increased labor supply by older workers boosts income before taxes and transfers. The only exception is in alternative 3, in which delayed retirement among older workers initially increases unemployment among higher-earning, younger workers. By 2015, even before the economy is assumed to return to full employment, all three simulations show gains in per capita income before taxes and transfers compared with the baseline. Small initial income gains grow as the simulated increase in delayed retirement increases. By 2040 increased labor supply boosts average per capita pretax, pretransfer income by nearly 1.6 percent under all three alternative simulations compared with the baseline. This relatively small change in aggregate per capita income masks notable increases for particular groups. For example, among 65–69-year-olds in 2040, average per capita income is projected to increase by 9.4 percent (see figure 3-3). Among those with low baseline incomes, the income increase is dramatically higher—more than 50 percent for people age 60 to 64 who are in the bottom income quintile in baseline, largely because they are assumed not to work in the baseline but then enter the labor force in the alternative simulations. Turning a

Table 3-7. *Average Change and Percent Change in Per Capita Income, Taxes and Premiums, and Net Income among Adults Age 25 and Older for Selected Years by Simulation*

Simulation	Year						
	2010	2015	2020	2025	2030	2035	2040
Average per capita income ($2,010)[a]							
Change (Alt - Baseline)							
Alt1	39	241	320	483	616	733	920
Alt2	0	49	315	467	600	717	910
Alt3	−12	31	309	473	610	725	919
Percent change							
Alt1	0.10	0.55	0.68	0.97	1.18	1.33	1.59
Alt2	0.00	0.11	0.67	0.94	1.15	1.31	1.57
Alt3	−0.03	0.07	0.65	0.95	1.17	1.32	1.59
Average per capita taxes and premiums ($2,010)[b]							
Change (Alt - Baseline)							
Alt1	13	71	98	166	217	280	346
Alt2	0	15	100	160	213	277	343
Alt3	−2	−6	96	165	218	278	345
Percent change							
Alt1	0.16	0.60	0.75	1.16	1.36	1.59	1.80
Alt2	0.00	0.13	0.76	1.11	1.33	1.57	1.78
Alt3	−0.02	−0.05	0.73	1.15	1.36	1.58	1.79
Average per capita net income ($2,010)[c]							
Change (Alt - Baseline)							
Alt1	27	171	222	316	397	453	575
Alt2	0	34	215	307	385	440	568
Alt3	−9	38	213	307	392	447	574
Percent change							
Alt1	0.09	0.53	0.65	0.90	1.10	1.21	1.49
Alt2	0.00	0.11	0.63	0.87	1.06	1.18	1.47
Alt3	−0.03	0.12	0.62	0.87	1.08	1.20	1.49

Source: Authors' tabulations from DYNASIM3.

a. Per capita income includes earnings, Social Security, defined-benefit pensions, asset income (interest, dividend, rental income, defined-contribution withdrawals), and SSI. Amounts are in 2010 CPI-adjusted dollars.

b. Per capita taxes and premiums include federal income tax, payroll tax, and Medicare premiums, less Medicare premium subsidies. Amounts are in 2010 CPI-adjusted dollars.

c. Per capita net income includes earnings, Social Security, defined-benefit pensions, asset income (interest, dividend, rental income, defined-contribution withdrawals), and Supplemental Security Income less federal income tax, payroll tax, and Medicare premiums less Medicare subsidies. Amounts are in 2010 CPI-adjusted dollars.

Figure 3-3. *Percent Change in Average Before-Tax per Capita Income in 2040 among Adults Age 25 and Older by Age and Baseline per Capita Income Quintile*

Percent

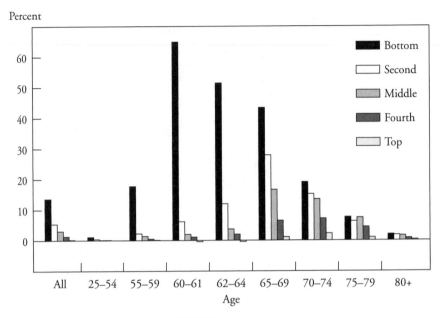

Source: Authors' tabulations from DYNASIM3.

nonworker into a worker typically improves annual income substantially. The net effect on households depends not only on earnings but also on taxes and transfers, which also change when labor supply increases.

Combining the income and tax changes, compared with the baseline, increased labor force participation among older workers will likely increase per capita net income among adults ages 25 and older by about 1.5 percent in aggregate by 2040 in all three of our alternative simulations (bottom panel of table 3-7). As with total income, the relatively small changes in aggregate per capita net income mask significant increases in per capita net income among the older workers who are delaying retirement. After accounting for taxes and transfers, increased labor force participation of older workers increases average net per capita income of 65–69-year-olds by 7.8 percent in 2040. Again, the gains are largest for older Americans with low baseline incomes (see figure 3-4).

Conclusions

Older Americans are working more today than the previous generation did a decade ago. This development reflects many influences: the increase in Social

Figure 3-4. *Percent Change in Average After-Tax per Capita Income in 2040 among Adults Age 25 and Older by Age and Baseline per Capita Income Quintile*

Percent

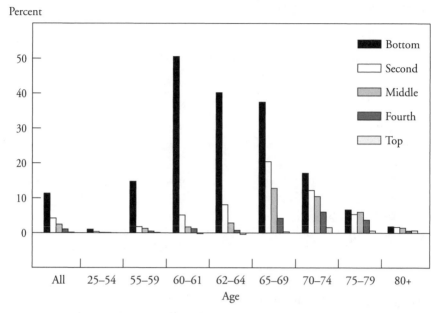

Source: Authors' tabulations from DYNASIM3.

Security's full-benefits age, the shift from defined-benefit to defined-contribution pensions, reduced retiree health insurance, and increases in educational levels of workers approaching traditional retirement age. If this trend continues, older workers will contribute to higher national output, reduce the growth of government spending, raise tax collections, and increase their own household incomes. These effects may not be immediate because current labor markets are weak. In fact, delayed retirement could decrease government revenues over the next few years if higher-skilled older workers displace lower-skilled younger workers. Eventually, however, increased labor force participation of older workers will unambiguously increase both government revenues and net household income at all ages. Our projections show that simulated increases in labor force participation could increase aggregate net government finances by more than 5 percent for the 2010 to 2040 year period.

The biggest gains will come to those with low incomes, who now tend to leave the labor force at relatively early ages. Non-Hispanic whites, well-educated, and high-income Americans already work at comparatively high rates and therefore gain comparatively little from increased labor supply at older ages. Early retirement is relatively prevalent among African Americans and Hispanics, those with limited education, and those with low incomes. Turning older nonworkers into workers can substantially increase net income. Furthermore, because these workers are typically in lower income tax brackets, they keep more of their increased labor income than upper-income workers do.

Although increased labor supply boosts total earnings, it lowers average earnings, which, in turn, slightly lowers projected Social Security benefits, which are tied to average earnings growth. For most beneficiaries, the gain in earnings, pensions, and asset income from working longer more than offsets the reduction in benefits.

In one respect, our simulations may underestimate the impact of increased labor supply. We project that new older workers work at the same wage rates and for the same annual hours as similar-aged workers who are employed in the baseline. We do not assume that those who are working in the baseline would also work longer. If older workers employed in the baseline increased work effort, the impact on earnings would increase.

We prepared our simulations before the 2012 year-end agreement to make permanent most of the tax provisions enacted under the administration of President George W. Bush. Accordingly, our tax estimates are somewhat higher than would be generated had the tax law in effect in 2012 not been modified. That said, it is difficult to predict what income tax rates will be decades hence. Income projections are equally uncertain. Still, DYNASIM3, which starts its projections in 1993, generates nearly twenty years of projections that compare well with historic data. Thus we are confident that the model captures the most important demographic and economic trends. One additional qualification to our fiscal projections is worth emphasizing: DYNASIM3 projects spending under some, but not all, federal programs. Despite this gap, the model does project major sources of income and expenditures. The central findings are, we believe, quite robust: higher labor force participation by older Americans unambiguously increases household earnings and federal taxes and lowers federal spending. We do not project the impact on spending and revenues of state and local governments, but we believe that increased labor force participation would have effects similar to those on the federal budget.

COMMENT BY
EUGENE STEUERLE

The first three chapters examine one of the most important issues in planning for our long-term economic future—labor force participation. Oddly this issue is largely neglected in most policy debates. In budget policy, this area is one of very few where government can simultaneously increase output and spending in a progressive way without an increase in the taxes needed to support that spending. If labor supply increases, the nation gets additional work and larger output. More output means more income for workers. More income means more revenue at any given tax rate. With more revenue, government can pay for more spending at the same tax rates, or lower tax rates. And that total spending can be made more progressive in aggregate. Increased labor would give policymakers the options sorely lacking in today's budget world.

Although labor force participation and the related issue of retirement have broad significance, they typically arise only within the context of Social Security. Yet most discussions of Social Security reform ignore the impacts of such reforms on the larger economy and personal income. Typically neither the Social Security actuaries nor anyone else even estimates such numbers as changes in income tax revenues.

I have two main points. First, although chapter 3 provides considerably improved estimates on the increased labor force participation of older workers— and corresponding increases in personal incomes and revenues—I believe the authors still substantially underestimate just how much labor supply is likely to increase even if policy is unchanged. Most models estimate the labor force supply of older workers without adequate consideration of how the demand for older workers increases once the available supply of younger workers declines. Second, legislators and analysts who study the behavior of the elderly should distinguish between population aging that occurs because fertility has fallen and aging that comes because people are living longer. Aging caused by fertility declines helps us understand why labor force participation tends to rise when eventually a larger share of the population is in the later stages of life. Aging caused by declines in age-specific mortality rates, conversely, helps demonstrate that the population's capacity for work does not decline, nor does dependency increase, simply because over time more people exceed a particular chronological age. Indeed, people with life expectancies similar to today's older workers (for example, persons aged about 56½ in 1940 who had the same life expectancy as those aged 65 in 2013) used to work many more years than is now typical; and they did so at a time when jobs were more physically demanding and health-care support was not nearly as good as it is now

Why Future Labor Force Participation of Older Workers is Seriously Underestimated

Over the past quarter century analysts have consistently underestimated future labor force participation of older workers and have repeatedly raised those estimates as facts violated previous projections. I want to emphasize that looking only at forces affecting supply—such as Social Security replacement rates, the shift to defined-contribution pensions from defined-benefit pension plans, and health status—tells an incomplete story.[10]

Models based on supply-side forces ignore labor demand. If the proportion of the population that is "young" falls because of declines in fertility rates, the elderly share of the population increases. If employers cannot find younger workers, they will almost assuredly increase their demand for older workers. To see why such an outcome is virtually certain, start with an extreme case. If no more babies were born, everyone in the population would eventually become 65 or older. It would be senseless to project the demand for workers age 65 and older based on the demand for that same age group in previous times. Somebody would have to do the work necessary to supply consumers' demand for goods and services. Of course, babies are still being born, but fertility did fall by about one-third in the mid- to late 1960s relative to the previous post–World War II period.

When researchers try to estimate the patterns of work for older workers with little or no reference to the potential supply of workers of other ages, they fail to take account the mutual dependence of supply and demand. Although male labor supply fell during much of the last half of the twentieth century, at least until near its end, both women and younger people (in the latter case because of the baby boom) were flooding into the labor force. In fact, the employment-adult population ratio, with the exception of recessionary periods, increased fairly steadily over that half century. Labor demand was being met. Again, factors such as level of government-provided retirement and health benefits, easily financed because of increases in the numbers of tax-paying female and younger workers, did affect the labor force participation or supply of older workers, but they were not the only forces at play.

A number of years ago, when Social Security projections forecast little or no growth in labor force participation of older workers, I came to believe, largely because of this labor demand phenomenon, that the projections would be wrong and that work by older people would increase.[11]

Such increases did, in fact, occur (figure 3-5). From 1987 to 2012, the Social Security actuaries have steadily increased their estimates of labor force participation among 65–69-year-olds. Their calculations include shifts in factors affecting labor supply caused by factors such as changes in the Social Security earnings test; but I suggest that failure to account for labor demand is a primary cause of Social

---

10. A further discussion of this issue is at www.urban.org/UploadedPDF/412631-correcting-labor-supply-projections.pdf.

11. Steuerle and Carasso (2001).

Figure 3-5. *Male Labor Force Participation Rates: Trustees' Assumptions versus Actual, Ages 65–69*

Percent

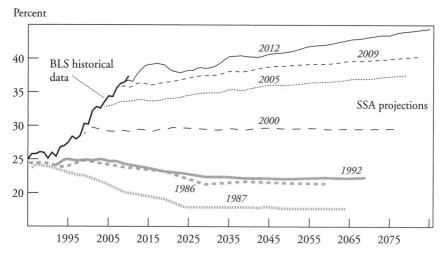

Source: Steuerle and Quakenbush (2012). Data from Bureau of Labor Statistics (BLS) and author's compilations of data from Social Security Actuary, Social Security Administration (SSA).

Security's need to constantly catch up with actual participation. Some developments that affect labor supply, such as the conversion from defined-benefit to defined-contribution pension plans, should not be considered as independent from labor demand, but rather partly as a natural response of employers to the need to retain older workers.

Dealing Accurately with "Aging" in Both Policy and Research

The term "aging" is misleading. Both policy discussions and research often go astray when they conflate two very different causes of an aging population: lower mortality and lower fertility rates.[12] First, we are living longer, which normally means the share of those over a given chronological age in the total population will tend to grow. However, the fact that a growing share of the population is over some age does not mean that a greater share of the population is in the last fourth or the last 10 percent of their adult lives, which is when needs for support or nec-

12. For this analysis, I ignore other factors such as immigration, economic cycles, and irregular changes in mortality and fertility trends.

essary dependency increase. It is more likely that increased longevity is correlated with improved health and with increased capability to work, even thrive, even with various impairments. Health science makes improvements along all these fronts (longevity, health, capability to cope with particular impairments) simultaneously. Therefore, when we try to measure the requirements for support in retirement, or the needs of an elderly population, whether public or private, what counts more is the proportion of the population that is within a certain number of years from death. One might also count the proportion in, say, the last 10 percent of their lives, though I am suspicious (and here provide no proof) that at the tail of the age distribution, those with equal remaining life expectancy across generations are more similar in terms of labor supply capability, along with mental and physical skills, than those with equal shares of life remaining.

Consider, for instance, a society in which life expectancy at age 65 was 75, and then a century later that life expectancy reaches 90. Would we consider the 65-year-old of each period, the one with a 10-year life expectancy and the one with a 25-year life expectancy, to be similar in health and needs and capabilities? Of course not. A more likely scenario would be that the 80-year-old of the more recent society would resemble the 65-year-old of a century before in many, though not all, characteristics.

The population is aging also because the birth rate is falling. By contrast with greater longevity, fewer children do mean that a greater share of the population will truly be in some last portion of their lives. In this case, a society will have to adjust to changing needs, at least to the extent that various impairments continue showing up more frequently in later years of life, or that fewer spouses are around to deal mutually with each other's impairments.

Within Social Security, this issue became especially salient when the baby boomers born between the end of World War II and the mid-1960s began moving into the over-62 population. Over the period from about 2008, when the first baby boomers turned 62, through the mid 2030s, the cost of Social Security measured as a share of gross domestic product (GDP) will rise by almost half, from 4.3 to 6.4 percent of GDP or from 11.6 to 17.4 percent of the taxable wage base.

If one fails to distinguish between the sources of "aging," one might conclude that there has been a steady increase in the percent of the population that is "aged." The percentage of the population aged 65 or older was 6.8 percent in 1940, became 12.7 percent in 2010, and will rise somewhat dramatically to 21.0 percent in 2040. But if one performs a similar calculation on the percentage of the population with a life expectancy equivalent to that of a 65-year-old in 1940, the figures become 6.8 percent in 1940, 7.2 percent in 2010, and 11.9 percent in 2040. Either way, there is substantial growth from 2010 to 2040, but the larger share of the growth in those considered "aged" over the 100-year period derives from a failure to adjust for life expectancy. What looked like a doubling from 1940 to 2010 on the basis of chronological age looks closer to zero growth on the basis of remaining life expectancy. Had an adjustment been made in retirement ages in Social Security—that is, had the number of years of promised benefits been held constant—there would be no projected long-term imbalance; indeed, annual benefits for the truly old could be maintained at a much higher level at today's tax rates.

U.S. public policy has not adequately adjusted to these important longevity and fertility changes. Congress tweaked Social Security in 1983 by raising what is called the "normal retirement age," but that is nothing more than a cut in annual benefits available to those who claim benefits at any given age.

The distinction between aging because of reduced fertility and aging because of an increase in life expectancy should affect not only policy considerations but also research. One should not treat 65-year-olds in 1940 as similar to 65-year-olds in 2040.[13] For research on capacity to work and many related subjects, one would probably be better off treating as alike people with similar life expectancies rather than people of similar chronological ages, at least in later years of life. If we want to know how the behavior of older workers evolves as their capacity to work declines, we need to determine when workers are equivalently "old." Many studies make a fundamental mistake when they treat people of the same chronological age at different dates as equally "old." At a minimum, they should test how results change depending on whether one uses chronological age or expected-years-until-death as the measure of age.

Some Policy Implications

What are the policy implications of these observations?

First, in estimating the impact of changes in Social Security policy that are expected to influence labor supply, analysts and policymakers should look beyond Social Security to how revenues and spending in all government accounts will change and to the effects on personal income and GDP. The first three chapters provide useful information that builds on previous work and similar conclusions by Barbara Butrica, Karen Smith, and me.[14]

13. For an example of how a measure of remaining life expectancy can affect research, see Cushing-Daniels and Steuerle (2007). Studies examining many behaviors of the "aged" over time, as well as trends in mortality rates, should also examine how results vary under different assumptions about who are equivalently aged in different time periods.

14. Butrica, Smith, and Steuerle (2006).

Second, retirement age should be related, at least in part, to the needs of people at different ages at each point in time. Social Security was set up mainly to help those no longer able to work, yet there is no evidence that the expansion of years of support met this criterion—or any other, as best I can tell, other than setting a fixed age parameter in the law. According to the Centers for Disease Control and Prevention, about 79 percent of those between the ages of 65 and 74 report being in good, very good, or excellent health, a figure not far removed from the 84 percent of 45–64 year-olds who report similar health status. It is hard to relate today's retirement ages and available years of retirement to the needs of either age group. Similarly, though one must be careful to distinguish among those with different capacities to work, the physical demands of jobs are not a reason to provide *everyone* more and more years of support over the decades; research shows clearly that such demands have declined, not increased.[15] Third, is adding another year to a retirement span that now approaches thirty years for a couple retiring at the earliest retirement age the highest and best use of limited government revenues, whatever tax rates one might otherwise support?[16] With growth in spending on health and retirement programs, along with interest payments, now scheduled to consume all or more than all of the growth in revenues that accompany future economic growth, one might conclude that increasing support for children's programs, work supports, or other investments might rank higher.

Summary

There is good news in all of this. Increased demand by employers for the services of older workers, combined with increased labor supply side by older age groups, provides tremendous potential for helping to maintain growth of national output and of revenues to support public programs.

I am optimistic also because it is misleading to suggest that living longer is equivalent to population aging. Decreased mortality generally does not imply population "aging" in terms of rising needs, whereas a declining birth rate generally does. Because the average age of retirement fell for the first decades of Social Security even as longevity was rising, the United States now has a pool of highly capable, knowledgeable, and savvy people in good, very good, and excellent health whose skills are underused. Older workers in the first half of the twenty-first century are a resource much as were women in the last half of the twentieth: the largest pool of underused human resources in our economy.

15. Steuerle, Spiro, and Johnson (1999).
16. See Steuerle (2011).

COMMENT BY
JOYCE MANCHESTER

Although I will comment as an independent researcher, not as a staff member of the Congressional Budget Office (CBO), I will put on my CBO hat just for a moment. The Congressional Budget Office has already incorporated about half of the labor supply increases that Gary Burtless has suggested into its baseline projections. At CBO we have thought carefully about how people will respond to the coming increase in the full-benefits age scheduled under current Social Security law. We have looked at how people responded to the increase in the full-benefits age from 65 to 66 and have projected a similar response when the full-benefits age goes from 66 to 67. This change bears on the question of how labor force participation of older people is likely to change between now and 2040. Burtless would extend the 1988–2010 trend into the future. The current CBO projection incorporates an increase in labor force participation by older Americans of about half of that size.[17] The result of more work at older ages is higher output, an improved outlook for Social Security, lower spending in programs such as the Supplemental Security Income (SSI) program, and other effects that reduce projected budget deficits. It also means more income for people in retirement.

Labor force participation rates for older men and women increased since the late 1980s for many reasons. Certainly the one-year increase in the full-benefits age under Social Security is one of the reasons. But other forces contributed to those trends as well. In 2000 the retirement earnings test was relaxed for people from 62 to the full-benefits age and was eliminated entirely for people older than the full-benefits age. The delayed retirement credit was increased to about 8 percent for each year benefit claiming is deferred. Many private employers have shifted from defined-benefit pensions to defined-contribution pensions and have curtailed or eliminated retiree health insurance. Those shifts tend to increase labor force participation rates at older ages. Educational attainment of successive cohorts of older workers has increased, and people with higher education tend to work longer. Successive cohorts of women have had an increasing attachment to the labor force over their careers. And, of course, longevity has risen, by about three years for men and about two and a half years for women.

Should we expect these factors to affect labor supply similarly in the future? The full-benefits age in Social Security is set to rise from 66 to 67; but that change will not be fully phased in until 2022 for workers reaching age 62, so that shift is some years away. Many analysts think that the switch from defined-benefit to

---

17. For further discussion on how CBO models labor force participation of older people in the long run, see CBO (2013).

defined-contribution pensions and the decline of retiree health insurance will continue, although the timing is unclear. Educational attainment seems to have plateaued. Cohort effects are uncertain. Labor force participation rates of women aged 25 to 55 seem to have leveled off. Longevity is likely to continue rising. The Social Security actuaries project that by 2040 life expectancy at age 65 will increase about two years for men and about one and a half years for women. Even so, the correlation of labor force participation with longevity is not well understood.

I believe that the evidence is quite strong that further increases in the full-benefits eligibility age under Social Security will lead to higher labor force participation. The other factors are likely to have less impact in the future than they did in the past.

One basic question is whether we should expect older people to work longer as longevity rises. Based on data from twelve Organization for Economic Cooperation and Development (OECD) countries over the past forty or fifty years, Kevin Milligan and David Wise (2012) found no solid evidence linking longevity and retirement ages. However, they found that retirement incentives from public pension programs powerfully influenced the timing of retirement and that recent reforms have been leading to more work at older ages. Of course, it may be that greater longevity is leading to changes in public policy, but they think that it is changes in public policy that are causing changes in the labor supply at older ages.

The evidence that increases in Social Security's full-benefits age from 65 to 66 has caused people to defer claiming benefits is quite clear. The ages at which people actually claim benefits have quite clearly moved up with the increases in the full-benefits age. To be sure, the ages at which people retire and claim Social Security benefits are not exactly linked, but they are closely correlated. At CBO we used this correlation to infer increases in labor force participation. We looked at data from the Current Population Survey[18] to give us an idea of the relationship between those two factors. Figures 3-6 and 3-7 show the age at which men and women actually claim Social Security benefits. One peak is at age 62. A second peak comes at or just after age 65. This second peak has moved up more or less in step as the full-benefits age increased from 65 to 66. As the full-benefits age rose in two-month steps, from 65 to 65 and 2 months, then to 65 and 4 months, and so forth, each cohort affected by those increases raised the second peak at the new full-benefits age and the age of claiming kept moving up.

It is unlikely that the trend to later retirement evident since the late 1980s will continue with the same slope through 2040. The full-benefits age will increase

18. The Current Population Study, sponsored by the U.S. Census Bureau and the U.S. Bureau of Labor Statistics (BLS), is the primary source of labor force statistics for the population of the United States.

Figure 3-6. *Ages at Which American Men Claim Social Security Benefits as Retired Workers, 1936–42*

Number

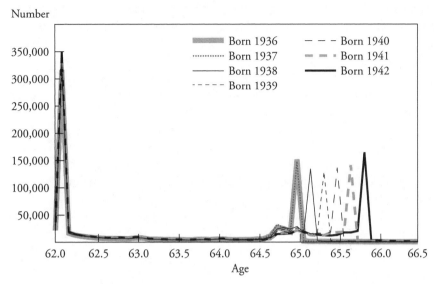

Source: Song and Manchester (2008).

Figure 3-7. *Ages at Which American Women Claim Social Security Benefits as Retired Workers, 1936–42*

Number

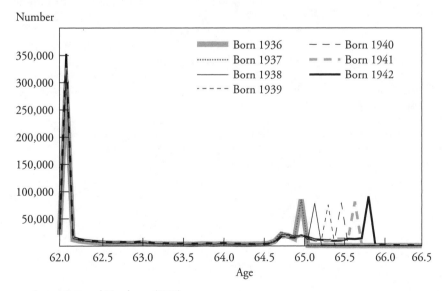

Source: Song and Manchester (2008).

another year from 66 to 67, affecting workers who reach age 62 from 2022 through 2027, and that will boost somewhat the age at which people claim Social Security and when they retire. But the other forces driving up retirement ages are mostly in the past. That is why I believe that it is reasonable to project some additional increases in retirement ages, but not at the same rates as in the past couple of decades.

If one accepts this projection, the effects on government finances and individual resources in retirement will be about half as large as those in the projections in chapter 3. In the CBO macro model, a change in the size of the labor force translates into a similar change in GDP because we project that labor and capital will grow at similar rates over time. A 1 percent increase in the labor force leads to about a 1 percent increase in GDP and to a 1 percent increase in revenues. Roughly 25 cents of each dollar of GDP goes to federal government revenues, at the margin.

Were the full-benefits age for Social Security to be increased still further—say, to age 70—there would be a further increase in labor force, GDP, and federal revenues.

References

Butrica, Barbara, Karen Smith, and Eugene Steuerle. 2006. "Working for a Good Retirement." The Retirement Project Discussion Papers Series. Washington, D.C.: Urban Institute.

Butrica, Barbara, Richard Johnson, Karen Smith, and Eugene Steuerle. 2004. "Does Work Pay at Older Ages?" Working Paper 2004-30. Chestnut Hill, Mass.: Center for Retirement Research at Boston College.

Board of Trustees. 2011. "The 2011 Annual Report of the Board of Trustees of the Federal Old-Age and Survivors Insurance and Federal Disability Insurance Trust Funds." Washington, D.C.: Social Security Administration (www.socialsecurity.gov/OACT/TR/2011/tr2011.pdf).

CBO (Congressional Budget Office). 2013. "How Will Older People's Participation in the Labor Force Be Affected by the Coming Increase in the Full Retirement Age for Social Security?" January (www.cbo.gov/publication/43834).

Cushing-Daniels, Brendan, and C. Eugene Steuerle. 2007. "Retirement and Social Security: A Time Series Approach Based on Remaining Life Expectancy." Washington, D.C.: Urban Institute (www.urban.org/UploadedPDF/412201-retirement-and-social-security.pdf).

Milligan, Kevin S., and David A. Wise. 2012. "Health and Work At Older Ages: Using Mortality To Assess Employment Capacity Across Countries." Working Paper 18229. Cambridge, Mass.: National Bureau of Economic Research, July (www.nber.org/papers/w18229.pdf).

Smith, Karen E., and Richard W. Johnson. 2013. "Impact of Higher Retirement Ages on Public Budgets: Simulation Results from DYNASIM3." Washington, D.C.: Urban Institute.

Song, Jae, and Joyce Manchester. 2008. "Have People Delayed Claiming Retirement Benefits? Responses to Changes in Social Security Rules." Working Paper 2008-03. Washington D.C.: Congressional Budget Office (www.cbo.gov/publication/19575).

Steuerle, Eugene. 2011. "The Progressive Case against Subsidizing Middle-Age Retirement." Washington, D.C.: Urban Institute (www.urban.org/publications/901414.html).

Steuerle, Eugene, and Adam Carasso. 2001. "A Prediction: Older Workers Will Work More in the Future." Washington, D.C.: Urban Institute (www.urban.org/UploadedPDF/Straight 32.pdf).

Steuerle, Eugene, and Caleb Quakenbush. 2012. "Correcting Labor Supply Projections for Older Workers Could Help Social Security and Economic Reform." Washington, D.C.: Urban Institute.

Steuerle, Eugene, Christopher Spiro, and Richard W. Johnson. 1999. "Can Americans Work Longer?" Straight Talk on Social Security No. 5. Washington, D.C.: Urban Institute (www.urban.org/UploadedPDF/Straight5.pdf).

4

Nudged, Pushed, or Mugged: Policies to Encourage Older Workers to Retire Later

HENRY J. AARON

Policies to encourage people to defer retirement are increasingly attractive for several reasons. Life expectancy is rising. Projected increases in budget deficits are traceable largely to anticipated growth of spending on pension and health benefits for the elderly and disabled. Within the federal budget, social insurance trust funds have their own funding gaps.

Increasing the labor supply of older people and those with impairments would ameliorate each of these challenges, provided that such increases can be achieved at reasonable cost. Delays in retirement may even be good for the health of those affected.[1] The policy challenge is to identify services that will enable the elderly and the impaired to remain economically active and to design incentives for them to do so. The danger is that such policy suggestions, often advanced by incumbents of sedentary jobs, will inflict serious inconvenience or genuine hardship on those for whom continued work imposes serious burdens or is downright impossible.

No social program precisely reaches all intended beneficiaries and no others. Typically, programs miss some putative targets and serve some unintended beneficiaries. Such incompleteness and inaccuracy arise both when new programs are introduced and when old programs are changed. However, inaccurate targeting is viewed differently for new and old programs. If a new program misses worthy ben-

---

1. Salhgren (2012), Dhaval, Rashad, and Spasojevic (2006), and Behncke (2009) reach similar results as do Coe and others (2010) and Rohwedder and Willis (2010). Other investigators have found that retirement is neutral or even beneficial to the retiree's health. See Bound and Waidmann (2007), Kerwin Kofi (2002), and Coe and Lindeboom (2008).

eficiaries and helps some who are not worthy, the inaccuracy is typically regarded as regrettable but inevitable. Conversely, withdrawing benefits from existing needy beneficiaries is often regarded as politically intolerable. This phenomenon has been observed in many contexts. Kahneman and Tversky built their theory of loss aversion around a related insight.[2] Charles Schultze articulated a similar principle in his political version of the Hippocratic Oath—"do not be seen to do obvious harm."[3] Changes in programs that benefit the retired, impaired, or elderly are definitely subject to this problem. Yet because no set of characteristics neatly distinguishes various classes of beneficiaries—the disabled versus nondisabled, early retirees versus late retirees—even the most carefully designed benefit cuts will harm some needy beneficiaries, and even the most carefully designed benefit liberalization will help some unintended recipients. A series of tables showing the only slightly different characteristics of those who claim benefits at various ages appears in the appendix to this chapter.[4]

Two other factors further complicate the task of reducing the growth of social insurance spending. Life expectancy has increased more among some groups than among others and not at all for some. The well-educated and those with comparatively high earnings have enjoyed sizeable increases in life expectancy.[5] Those with comparatively low education and earnings have experienced little or no increase in life expectancy. In designing incentives to encourage older workers to delay retirement, it is important to keep in mind that older Americans work more than do adults of the same age in most other developed countries.

Movements in the U.S. labor supply have been the result of strongly offsetting trends among men and women (table 4-1). From 1950 through 1990 labor supply by men under age 65 fell slightly, but among men over age 65 it fell sharply. Overall, the proportion of men age 16 and over who were *not* working for pay or looking for work rose from 13.7 percent in 1950 to 23.6 percent in 1990. However, overall the labor supply increased as younger women flooded into paid work outside the home. Overall the share of Americans age 16 or older *not* in the labor force fell from 40.8 percent in 1950 to 33.5 percent in 1990.

Starting around 1990, many of these trends shifted. Labor force participation by older men began to increase, even as the proportion of younger men in the labor force continued to fall. Decades of rapidly rising female labor force participation

2. Kahneman and Tversky (1979).

3. Schultze (1977), p. 70.

4. Tables 4A-1 through 4A-7 are drawn from Aaron and Callan (2011) and document that the characteristics of those who retire from work at each age and those who continue to work at the same age overlap to a remarkable degree. A model that incorporates many of these characteristics is also incapable of distinguishing those who will retire from those who will continue working with any significant predictive value.

5. Waldron (2007a and 2007b). See also Olshansky and others (2012).

Table 4-1. *U.S. Labor Force Participation Rates*

	1950	1990	2010	2035
Males				
16–44	.907	.876	.823	.839
45–64	.918	.806	.787	.759
65+	.458	.163	.221	.226
16+	.863	.764	.723	.687
Females				
16–44	.387	.714	.683	.723
45–64	.332	.593	.661	.616
65+	.097	.086	.143	.166
16+	.339	.575	.580	.562
All				
16–44	.636	.794	.753	.781
45–64	.621	.695	.722	.686
65+	.267	.118	.177	.193
16+	.592	.665	.650	.623

Source: Goss (2010).

ended; overall labor force activity by women changed little between 1990 and 2010. A small drop in the proportion of younger women in the labor force was offset by a near doubling of labor force participation by older women.

Past trends in labor supply do not foretell future shifts. The Social Security Administration (SSA) projects some drop in labor force participation by both men and women between 2010 and 2035 (table 4-1). Most of that drop results from population aging. Within broad age groups, the SSA projects little change in labor participation rates by men or women. In particular, the SSA's projections assume that the sharp increase in paid work by people over age 65 that occurred between 1990 and 2010 will end.

Other chapters explore the economic implications if the labor supply continues to increase over the next couple of decades. More workers than assumed by Social Security's actuaries means perceptibly more gross domestic product (GDP) and tax revenue and less public spending on health and pension benefits than the actuaries project. Whether these changes will be realized depends on whether the increase in labor force participation by older men and women that started a couple of decades ago continues. The behavioral shifts emerged for various reasons.[6] Employers froze or replaced most defined-benefit private plans with defined-contribution plans. Defined-benefit plans contain strong retirement incentives

6. Munnell and Sass (2007).

after workers reach certain ages or achieve particular tenure thresholds that defined-contribution plans do not. The shift of employment from hard physical jobs to less onerous work continued. The delayed retirement credit—the increase in the annual benefit paid to those who wait until older ages to claim Social Security—was increased. The retirement test—the reduction in benefits paid to people who worked after the full-benefits age—was ended. Two stock market collapses made retirement less affordable for many. Successive cohorts of older workers were better educated than those who preceded them; and labor force participation among older workers is positively related to education. Each of these developments is plausibly linked to an increase in labor supply. But their absolute impact and relative importance are not known with any precision. Sorting out the relative influence of these factors is even harder because peer group effects on retirement decisions are also important and evolve slowly over time. Because reliable estimates of how much each factor contributed to past labor force trends do not exist, confidence in predicting how fast or how much policy changes will alter labor supply in the future is unjustified.

This chapter reviews a partial list of policy changes that would shift incentives of older workers to remain economically active and of employers to hire them. It also offers some comments on distributional effects and administrative considerations. As Nicole Maestas emphasizes in her comments on this chapter, evaluation of each policy depends on how one weights various conflicting objectives—improving income for the elderly, closing funding gaps in social insurance trust funds, lowering projected budget deficits, and altering the distribution of incomes. It also depends on the weight one attaches to ending benefits that recipients expect versus raising taxes or cutting other government spending that reduces the well-being of others.

Increasing the Age for Benefits

Two commonly discussed changes in Social Security bear on labor supply by older workers. An increase in the "normal" retirement age would lower benefits across the board. An increase in the age of initial eligibility for retirement benefits would delay access to them. Some proposals would cut benefits selectively for comparatively high earners. I propose a hybrid measure: a selective decrease in pensions for workers with high earnings, but only if they claim benefits early.

Raising the "Normal" Retirement Age

The most commonly discussed change in Social Security is an increase in the "normal" retirement age, now 66. Based on current law, the "normal" retirement age will rise gradually by an additional year, reaching age 67 for workers born after

> Box 4-1. *Social Security Benefits at Ages 62, 66, and 70*
>
> The Social Security benefit payable to those who claim benefits at age 66 is 100 percent of the *primary insurance amount*—the benefit generated by the Social Security benefit formula. People who claim benefits before (or after) age 66 receive less (or more) than 100 percent of the primary insurance amount. Those who claim benefits at age 62—the youngest age at which retirement benefits are paid—now receive 75 percent of the age-66 benefit. Those who claim benefits at age 70 receive 132 percent of the age-66 benefit. There is no further increase for those who claim benefits after age 70 (unless earnings from added years of work raise the primary insurance amount). Benefits are increased approximately 8 percent for each year claiming is delayed after age 66 and are reduced approximately 6 2/3 percent for each year benefits are claimed earlier than age 66.

1960. Each year by which the "normal" retirement age is increased reduces benefits across the board for new claimants by about 8 percent (see box 4-1 for an explanation of the relationship between the age at which benefits are claimed and benefit amounts). The reduction in total spending starts small, because new claimants initially comprise a small fraction of all beneficiaries. As more and more claimants are subject to the cut, the budget savings grow and stabilize at about 8 percent of total benefits when all beneficiaries are eventually subject to the benefit reduction.

Calling age 66 the "normal" retirement age is inaccurate and fosters enormous confusion, even among "experts." Although it is true that the benefit formula pivots on pensions calculated for 66-year-olds, age 66 is not "normal" in any sense. More benefits are claimed at age 62 than at any other age. Eighty percent of newly awarded retirement benefits in 2011 went to people who applied before age 66. Nor is age 66 the age at which most people stop working—most retire before age 66. Raising the "normal" retirement age does not change the age at which benefits are first available, nor does it force any change in the date at which benefits are claimed. Increasing the "normal" retirement age simply cuts pensions *proportionately for all new beneficiaries*, regardless of the age at which they start receiving benefits. The name for this type of benefit cut suggests that it is linked to when people retire or when they can or do claim benefits, all of which is false.

Understanding would improve if Social Security were described as paying *full* benefits at age 70 and reduced benefits if one claims benefits at earlier ages.[7] What

---

7. Much the same improvement in understanding would result if age 62 were described as "the retirement age" with a bonus paid for each year claiming is delayed.

is now misleadingly called an increase in the "normal" retirement age would then be correctly labeled as an 8 percent cut in benefits regardless of when they are claimed.

The policy questions relate to whether such across-the-board cuts in Social Security benefits are a good way to close the gap in long-term funding that the program faces. Relevant policy questions include:

—Are across-the-board benefit cuts justified by increases in longevity?

—Would such cuts increase labor supply by older workers?

—How would reducing retirement benefits affect applications for Social Security Disability Insurance (SSDI) or Supplemental Security Income (SSI)?

—What would be the impact of a benefit cut on the balance between Social Security revenues and expenditures and on the overall budget?

—Would cutting retirement benefits cause hardship later for those who take reduced benefits soon after they are eligible if they later lose the capacity to supplement their pensions with part-time work and deplete other assets? If so, what could be done to relieve such hardships?

Increases in longevity boost program costs, because beneficiaries will receive pensions for more years if age of claiming is unchanged or increased annual benefits if the age of claiming rises with longevity. Whether this increased fiscal cost is or is not justified depends on whether benefit levels are regarded as adequate. From that standpoint, it is important to recognize that current U.S. benefits are lower than those of most other countries at similar levels of economic development (see table 4-2). The average present discounted value of lifetime Social Security benefits in the United States is 40 percent below the average of OECD countries. This computation takes account of when benefits are initially available, their size, and how they are taxed, as well as life expectancy. Annual benefits in the United States have been cut and will be cut further because of past legislation. Reducing benefits payable to all those claiming retirement benefits would offset some or all of the increased program costs.

Raising the "normal" or "full-benefits" age will delay retirement ages for two reasons. First, according to standard economic theory, the reduction in the present discounted value of lifetime benefits lowers each worker's lifetime wealth. Because of reduced lifetime wealth, workers will buy fewer goods, including "leisure," of which time spent in retirement is a part. Second, a boost in the "normal" or full-benefits age will act as a signal to some workers that the norm for retirement has increased.

The incentive to apply for SSDI benefits would be increased because those declared disabled receive benefits equal to those payable at the full-benefits age, while those who claim early retirement benefits receive reduced benefits for the rest of their lives.

Table 4-2. *International Comparison of Retirement Pension Levels: Gross Replacement Rates and Penson Wealth*

| Country | Average earners (Ratio to earnings) | | All earners (U.S. dollars) |
	Gross replacement rate[a]	Net pension wealth[b]	Average pension wealth[c]
Netherlands	0.88	13.2	744,000
Spain	0.81	11.0	541,000
Austria	0.81	7.3	512,000
Denmark	0.80	8.4	744,000
Italy	0.68	7.9	607,000
Sweden	0.62	7.6	487,000
Norway	0.59	9.2	462,000
Switzerland	0.58	8.7	487,000
Finland	0.56	7.3	414,000
France	0.53	8.8	426,000
Canada	0.44	7.3	355,000
Germany	0.43	6.3	318,000
Australia	0.42	7.3	363,000
Belgium	0.42	6.2	293,000
New Zealand	0.39	6.4	410,000
United States	0.39	6.0	264,000
Japan	0.34	5.5	266,000
United Kingdom	0.31	4.3	210,000
Weighted OECD average[d]	0.59	8.6	442,000

Source: OECD 2009.

a. Gross replacement rate is the ratio of the pension to average earnings.

b. Net pension wealth is a simple unweighted average of the values reported for men and for women.

c. Average pension wealth is expressed in U.S. dollars at official exchange rates.

d. Weighted OECD averages include countries excluded from the table.

Many analysts have become concerned that raising the "normal" or full-benefits age without also increasing the age of initial entitlement would create a serious risk that people who claim benefits early, when they can supplement Social Security with part-time earnings or other assets, but would then find themselves impoverished later when work is no longer possible and other savings have been depleted.

Raising the Age of Initial Eligibility

Some current deficit-reduction plans propose not only to cut benefits across the board by raising the "normal" retirement age, but also to raise the age at which retirement benefits can first be claimed. Unlike increases in the "normal" retirement age, raising the age at which benefits can initially be claimed lowers Social Security outlays only temporarily, but raises long-term program costs. The short-term savings are obvious. The long-term increases result because the increase in annual benefits paid to those who delay claiming now roughly offsets the reduction in duration of benefits.[8] Raising the age of initial eligibility will cause some who are denied early retirement benefits to apply for and receive SSDI benefits. Disability benefits are the same amount as retirement benefits would be if claimed at the full-benefits age, which is to say that they are higher than early retirement benefits. Those higher disability benefits continue until the worker dies. In addition, the worker's survivors will receive benefits based on the worker's primary insurance amounts, not on the reduced benefits that would be used if the worker claimed retirement benefits before the full-benefits age.

Based on standard economic theory, raising the age of initial eligibility would slightly increase labor supply. Workers with insufficient liquid assets or income to support themselves will find that they need to work somewhat longer if the age of initial eligibility is increased. Otherwise, raising the age of initial eligibility should not affect the retirement decision of the average worker because subsequent benefit increases more than compensate workers on the average for the delay in their pensions. As with changes in the "normal" or full-benefits age, raising the age of initial entitlement might well influence labor supply because it sends a signal that public policy has endorsed or recommended that retirement should be delayed.

The Congressional Budget Office reported a calculation suggesting that raising the age of initial eligibility by one year would boost labor supply more than would the benefit cut represented by raising the "normal" retirement age by one year.[9] Alan Gustman and Thomas Steinmeier estimate that raising the age of initial eligibility by two years would increase labor supply by about 12 percent among workers aged 62 to 64, but have no effect at other ages.[10] They estimate that the decision to raise the "normal" retirement age from 65 to 67 increased labor supply by variable amounts averaging somewhat more than 1 percent for workers from age 61 to 67. The fact that roughly a fifth of retirees depend exclusively on Social Security and roughly three-fifths receive more than half their income from Social Security suggests that raising the age of initial eligibility could strongly encourage continued labor supply by people with little unearned income from sources other than Social Security.

8. Shoven and Slavov (2012). See also Munnell (2012).
9. Myerson and Manchester (2012).
10. Gustman and Steinmeier (2012).

Policy Considerations

Some workers rationally claim benefits early—for example, single workers who are terminally ill. But for many, early claiming is a myopic mistake. Most workers who want to retire and have sufficient non–Social Security assets or income to support themselves stand to gain financially by delaying claiming their retirement benefits as long as possible.[11] They are better off spending down other assets because Social Security provides a real rate of return of 7–8 percent in the form of an increase in a riskless, fully price-indexed annuity. Few private investments offer similar returns.

Concern that meager benefits would leave early claimants impoverished as they age has led various commissions and study groups to try to target benefit cuts to those best able to shoulder them. One approach is to cut Social Security benefits for all, but provide "safety valve" benefits to workers for whom continued employment creates serious hardships. Another approach is to target cuts only to workers with comparatively high earnings.

Safety Valve Benefits

Increasing the age of eligibility for Social Security will reduce budget outlays for many years. Is it possible to increase the age of eligibility in ways that protect those for whom delay or reduction in Social Security retirement benefits will cause hardship? One way would be to spare those for whom retirement is urgent. Another would be to provide compensating access to other benefits. Screens must be sufficiently *sensitive,* that is in identifying a large proportion of those who are intended beneficiaries, and *specific,* that is in not helping large numbers who are not intended beneficiaries. No available screen comes close to perfection on both scores. The policy challenge is to find safety-valve benefits that are "good enough."

ACCESS TO SOCIAL SECURITY DISABILITY INSURANCE.   One study reported that roughly 12 percent of those who claimed Social Security benefits before age 65 satisfied all requirements for eligibility for disability coverage (under either Social Security or SSI) other than "continuity of work."[12] Eligibility for SSDI hinges on a recency-of-work requirement—workers must have had earnings subject to the payroll tax in five of the preceding ten years. This requirement differs from, and is generally stricter than, that for retirement benefits: work subject to the payroll tax in at least ten years over one's entire life. The same study reports that an additional 13 percent of early claimants have health problems that impair their ability to

11. Shoven and Slavov (2012).
12. Leonesio, Vaughn, and Wixon (2003).

work. Eliminating the recency-of-work requirement at age 62 would enable a minority of those who claim benefits early to qualify for SSDI benefits rather than retirement benefits. Because disability benefits are higher than early retirement benefits and continue as long as the beneficiary lives, access to disability benefits would be a benefit increase for affected workers and their survivors. This policy shift would provide no relief for the remaining 88 percent of early claimants, some of whom doubtlessly claim early retirement benefits for compelling reasons.

INCREASED ASSET AND INCOME THRESHOLDS UNDER SUPPLEMENTAL SECU-RITY INCOME.   Among those who now claim Social Security benefits at age 62 or soon thereafter are some with incomes and assets low enough to qualify for SSI. Currently, one must be at least age 65 to qualify for SSI unless one is disabled. Lowering the age of eligibility for SSI to 62 would provide income to those for whom the need to retire is great. Maximum SSI benefits are low—$710 a month in 2013 for single persons and $1,066 for couples. Actual benefits often turn out to be even lower because of offsets. Benefits are reduced dollar for dollar for unearned income over $20 a month and by $1 for every $2 of earnings over $65 per month ($85 if there is no unearned income). Only a small proportion of Social Security recipients qualify for SSI because Social Security benefits typically render people ineligible for SSI. But more than half of elderly SSI recipients also receive Social Security.

Reducing access to Social Security by raising the age of eligibility for benefits would increase the pool of people with incomes low enough to qualify for SSI. But many who are income eligible would still not qualify because of SSI's strict asset limits—$2,000 for single persons and $3,000 for couples. Those limits have not been increased in twenty-three years. Had asset limits been indexed for prices, they would now be approximately $3,700 for individuals and $5,600 for couples. Had they been indexed to per capita GDP, the limits would be approximately $4,600 for individuals and $6,900 for couples.

By either comparison, it is clear that an asset limit, already stringent in 1989, has been drastically cut. Justifications for such a cut are hard to imagine. Because of the recent surge in long-term unemployment, now would be a good time to raise the asset limits for SSI for the general population. An even larger step-up or complete elimination of the asset limit for those who would be disadvantaged by an increase in the age of eligibility for Social Security would also be a highly specific way to help this group. The Affordable Care Act has eliminated the asset test for Medicaid eligibility. The current SSI benefit would be lower than the Social Security retirement pension of most workers. Still, if the age at which Social Security benefits can be claimed is raised from age 62, access to SSI would provide relief to those with little other income.

Lowering the age of eligibility for SSI would provide workers with low earnings a double dividend—they would receive SSI retirement benefits that would be higher in some cases than the early-retiree Social Security benefits *and* they would receive unreduced Social Security benefits when they reach the full-benefits age.

Targeted Benefit Cuts

Instead of cutting Social Security benefits across the board and providing back-up coverage for those who would suffer most from those cuts, some plans call for selective cuts targeted to comparatively high earners.

PROGRESSIVE INDEXING.   The current Social Security benefit formula provides larger benefits in relation to earnings for low earners than for high earners. Earnings up to a certain point generate 90 cents in benefits per dollar of average earnings. For an additional range, earnings generate 32 cents in benefits per dollar of earnings. Above this second range, earnings generate 15 cents in benefits per dollar of earnings. The points at which these percentages apply are known as "bend points." The bend points are adjusted annually by the percentage change in average earnings, a practice called "wage indexing." This practice ensures that over time most workers at any given *relative* position in the earnings distribution receive pensions that replace approximately the same ratio of their average earnings.

Over the years, some have proposed that the bend points be adjusted for changes in prices, rather than wages. This practice would hold approximately constant over time the ratio of benefits to earnings for workers at any given *absolute* position in the earnings distribution. Because prices normally rise less than average wages, "price indexing"—adjusting the bend points for price changes—would generate lower benefits than wage indexing does, as it would shrink the range of earnings to which the 90 percent and 32 percent benefit replacement ranges apply and increase the proportion of earnings to which the 15 percent replacement rate applies.

Increasing longevity raises the discounted present value of benefits. The largest recent increases in longevity have accrued to people with comparatively high earnings (and education, which is correlated with earnings). For these and perhaps other reasons, some analysts have suggested that wage indexing be limited to the lower part of the earnings distribution and that price indexing of Social Security retirement and disability benefits be applied above certain earnings, a policy known as "progressive price indexing." The original proposal would have applied price indexing above the 30th percentile of the earnings distribution. Subsequent versions would start price indexing farther up the earnings distribution—at the 40th, 50th, or 60th earnings percentile. Still other proposals would directly lower

Table 4-3. *Illustrative Benefit Impacts of Cutting Benefits for Early Claimants*

Age of claiming	Average annual earnings (U.S. dollars)						
	57,066	60,000	70,000	80,000	90,000	100,000	106,800
	Percent change in benefits						
62	0	1.8	7.4	12.4	16.9	20.9	23.5
63	0	1.2	5.0	8.6	11.7	14.5	16.3
64	0	0.9	3.5	6.0	8.2	10.1	11.4
65	0	0.6	2.5	4.2	5.7	7.1	8.0
66 or later	0	0	0	0	0	0	0

Source: Author's calculations.

the replacement rates applicable in the upper earnings range from 15 to 10 percent or even less.

All such proposals lower benefits selectively for workers in income ranges where most longevity increases have occurred. All of these plans would reduce the projected long-term imbalance in the Social Security trust funds. By lowering benefit *levels* payable at any age, such reductions would modestly discourage workers from retiring early. But they would not change the *relative* benefits paid to workers who retire at one age or another.

SELECTIVE REDUCTION IN EARLY RETIREMENT BENEFITS. Under an alternative approach, Congress could cut benefits selectively for people with comparatively high average earnings who claim benefits at age 62 or soon thereafter. This change in the benefit formula is intended primarily to encourage workers to defer retirement. Table 4-3 illustrates one such formula. The benefit formula would be unchanged for any worker who claims benefits at age 66 or later. No worker who claims benefits at age 62 would receive a pension larger than that paid to a worker at the 70th percentile in the earnings distribution at age 62. The average indexed annual earnings amount at the 70th percentile in 2011 was $57,066. The benefits for workers with average earnings above the 70th percentile who claim benefits between age 62 and age 66 would be a linear interpolation between the benefits payable at age 62 and those payable on the worker's own average indexed annual earnings history at age 66.

Clearly, this general approach could be applied in different ways. The percentile in the earnings distribution could be higher or lower than the 70th percentile. Those with earnings above the chosen level who retire at age 62 could be denied part rather than all of the extra benefit their earnings provide. The age at which the penalty for early retirement ends could differ. For example, benefits of only workers who claim benefits before, say, age 65 could be reduced, or reductions could apply to all workers who claim benefits before age 70. The earnings threshold to which the penalty applies could continue to be wage indexed, or it could be price indexed so that it applies to a growing share of the workforce over time.

These choices would affect both the size of the incentive and the number of claimants to whom the incentive to delay claiming would apply. The common characteristic of all such plans is that they increase the financial incentive to wait to claim benefits by abandoning the principle that the benefit formula should be neutral or close to neutral with respect to the timing of retirement.

This approach has shortcomings. It is complex. It would reduce benefits not only for those who can easily defer benefit claiming but also for those whose need to claim benefits is exigent. This approach is more than a nudge to delay claiming, but less than flat denial of benefits at early ages.

This change in the benefit formula would reduce Social Security benefits to the extent that it *fails* to cause workers to retire later. If every worker to whom the early retirement penalty applied chose, and was able, to work long enough to avoid the penalty, Social Security spending would actually increase because the current formula provides a somewhat larger-than-actuarially-fair benefit increase for delaying benefit claims and because some would be induced to claim SSDI. The spending increase could be larger because not all workers would benefit equally from deferring when they claim benefits. If the workers who stand to gain most were more likely to wait than those who gain little, or those who actually suffer losses from waiting (for example, because of short life expectancies), the increase in the cost of Social Security would go up. In that event, however, the labor force, potential GDP, and personal and corporation income taxes would all be increased at full employment, as indicated by the estimates in chapters 1–3.

Data from the University of Michigan's Health and Retirement Study (with Social Security earnings and benefit information linked) permit one to see the difference between the characteristics of those with average earnings above and below the 70th percentile (see table 4-4).[13] The correlations between earnings and a wide range of personal and economic characteristics are all unsurprising, but the distributions overlap. A larger proportion of those with comparatively high incomes than of those with comparatively low incomes would be able to delay claiming benefits (because their wealth permits some delay) and a smaller proportion is impaired or working in burdensome jobs. But no cutoff point supports policies that are either specific or sensitive. Some people with comparatively high average earnings have meager assets, some work in difficult jobs requiring heavy physical or mental effort, and so on.

---

13. University of Michigan's Health and Retirement Study is a longitudinal panel study that surveys a representative sample of more than 26,000 Americans over the age of 50 every two years. It is supported by the National Institute on Aging and the Social Security Administration.

Table 4-4. Characteristics of People above and below the 70th Percentile of Average Earnings

Characteristic	Earnings at 70th percentile or above	Earnings below 70th percentile
	Percent of group with each characteristic	
Education, high school or less	11.4	28.8
Self-reported health, fair or poor	9.5	18.4
Self-reported health change, somewhat or much worse	15.2	17.5
Health limits work	11.0	18.2
Limits on one or more activities of daily living	3.2	7.3
Limits on one or more instrumental activities of daily living	3.1	3.7
One or more functional limitations: walk one block; climb stairs; lift and carry 10 pounds	17.4	23.0
Mental health		
No reported problems	64.9	15.0
Two or more problems	48.5	26.8
Total wealth		
$50,000 or less	8.4	29.3
Job requires (all or most of the time)		
Physical effort	22.9	40.2
Lifting heavy loads	9.9	15.6
Stooping or crouching	15.9	27.7
Stress	49.3	50.4
Occupation		
Managerial or professional	41.2	18.9
"Hard" jobs	30.5	35.1

Source: Author's tabulations based on data from the Health and Retirement Study.

Payroll Taxes and Medicare

Social insurance rules could be altered to increase incentives for employment of older workers. Shoven and Shultz have proposed two such changes.[14] The Social Security payroll tax could be reduced or eliminated at a certain age, provided that workers had accumulated sufficient years of earnings credits. Zeroing out the entire tax would eliminate a 12.4-percentage-point wedge between the cost of employing such workers and the net income they receive. Standard economic theory holds that the payroll tax is borne by workers, whether levied on employers or employees. The findings of behavioral economics indicate that people may not always behave according to the principles assumed in standard economic theory. Those

14. Shoven and Shultz (2008).

findings suggest that different approaches to lowering the payroll tax for older workers might have different effects on their supply of labor and different effects on the demand for their services.[15] Thus, the tax could be eliminated selectively on workers or employers. Gustman and Steinmeier estimate that eliminating the payroll tax on a sample of married workers would raise the overall labor supply only negligibly, but would cause some substitution of work after age 65 for work before age 65.[16]

In either form, the proposal might enlarge the existing financial imbalance within the Social Security system. To the extent that it succeeded in boosting the overall labor force participation rate, it would generate added potential GDP and boost general revenues. Conditioning the tax cut on years of service would also provide greater relief for men than for women because women typically spend more years than men outside the paid labor force. In addition, the value of eliminating the tax would be larger for high than for low earners.

As a companion to this proposal, Shoven and Shultz propose a change in Medicare rules that would lower the cost of providing health coverage to many older workers.[17] Workers over age 65 are normally eligible for Medicare hospital insurance (part A), whether or not they are retired. But Medicare generally does not pay for services for employees who are covered by an employer-sponsored health insurance plan unless the employee works for a company covering twenty or fewer employees. Employees covered by an employer-sponsored plan have the option to buy into Supplemental Medical Insurance (SMI, or part B), but normally they do not purchase it because SMI coverage duplicates what they receive from their employers. Under the Shoven-Shultz proposal, Medicare would become the first payer for everyone over age 65. This shift in payment priority would relieve employers of the comparatively high average cost of insurance coverage for older workers. Once again, it is not clear whether the result would be somewhat increased wages for older workers, with an attendant boost in labor supply, or somewhat reduced per-worker employment expense, with attendant increase in demand by employers for the services of older workers.

This shift would deepen the gap between projected spending and revenues in the Medicare hospital insurance program and boost the general revenues required to support SMI. As with the other measures, to the extent that it boosts overall labor force participation, it would increase potential GDP and potential income and corporation taxes.

15. Atkinson (2012).
16. Gustman and Steinmeier (2012).
17. Shoven and Shultz (2008).

Disability Benefits

Several ill-coordinated private and public programs provide financial support, rehabilitative services, and health care to people who have impairments that make work difficult or impossible. These programs include disability benefits under Social Security and SSI, workers compensation, vocational rehabilitation, Medicaid, and private disability insurance. These programs have been criticized for various flaws, including perverse incentives, inconsistent standards, excessive administrative delay, and delivery of inappropriate services. At the same time, they provide an enormous amount of assistance to very needy people, an achievement not emphasized by some critics. Liebman and Smalligan expressed this duality at a Brookings conference in September 2012. After listing the problems with these programs and the need for research to improve program design and administration, they noted:

> SSDI is a system that largely works. We were impressed with the skills of the government workers involved in all steps of the process. . . . [I]t appeared that most of the time they were getting the decisions right. . . . In addition, the people we observed applying for benefits were almost always people in significant need of some type of service.[18]

Two underlying problems bedevil design of SSDI benefits. The first is that both the sources and nature of the impairments are enormously varied. Some impairments preclude work permanently and completely. Yet some fraction of people with many impairments, even very serious ones, do work. Second, the definition of disability—the incapacity to engage in meaningful economic activity—produces an inescapable dilemma. Either benefits stop when a person previously judged eligible to receive them has significant and sustained earnings—a financial disincentive to work—or benefits continue, thus generating a powerful incentive to get on the rolls by people who find themselves without earnings, whether or not they retain or could eventually regain the capacity to work. The unavoidable result is moral hazard of one kind or another. Furthermore, given the definition of disability, no administrative system, however scrupulous, can avoid some mix of false positives—approving people for services who have some capacity to work—and false negatives—denying assistance to those who should receive help. Spending more on administration can reduce errors of each kind, but administration is costly; beyond some point, accepting the errors is less costly than what it would take to eliminate them.

18. Liebman and Smalligan (2013).

Although the challenge of efficiently designing and administering assistance for those with impairments is daunting, most observers believe that the current system could be significantly improved. Services to help people with impairments regain or acquire the capacity to work often come with excessive delay. They are often not well-designed to restore their capacity to work, or even intended to do so. And they are linked to financial incentives that discourage work. The process by which eligibility for SSDI is determined is cumbersome, protracted, and costly. Critics agree that such delays sometimes undermine whatever capacity to work applicants retain. Applicants remain inactive out of fear that if they work while their applications are pending they will jeopardize their chances of qualifying for benefits. Far better than a long period of close-to-enforced idleness as a precondition for financial aid, health insurance, or rehabilitative services, which are then jeopardized by actual earnings, would be a process that speedily determined eligibility and that quickly provided services tailored to the specific problems of each applicant.

The source of benefits for those with impairments has been changing. The number of people eligible for disability benefits through Social Security and SSI has been rising for various reasons. Women increasingly have work histories that qualify them for SSDI, and they have a higher SSDI claiming incidence than do men. The average age of workers is rising, and the incidence of disability rises with age. But age-specific incidence of claiming has also been rising because of changes in both administrative practices and application behavior. Meanwhile, the number of people receiving benefits through workers compensation has been falling, a possible contributing factor in the growth of SSDI claims.

Many analysts agree that it would be possible to administer disability benefits more effectively. To do so would require both redesign of procedures and increased staff. Liebman and Smalligan claim that information is not yet adequate to identify which interventions and procedures would work best and whether such changes would cost more than they are worth.[19] Many of those who apply for disability benefits have personal characteristics, in addition to serious impairments, that lower their potential earnings.[20] It is not clear exactly how to design a system to identify those who have a good chance of returning to work with sufficient specificity to produce benefits greater than costs. To date, the increases in earnings resulting from programs intended to increase labor supply by those with impairments has been small enough so that the balance between costs and benefits is not clear. For that reason, Liebman and Smalligan propose pilots to test

---

19. Liebman and Smalligan (2013).
20. Kirk (2012).

alternative approaches. Others have suggested encouraging employers to help keep workers with impairments on the job by experience rating the payroll tax dedicated to SSDI or requiring employers to carry private disability insurance.[21]

The potential return from enabling those receiving disability benefits to resume paid work seems to be increasing. The average age of SSDI applicants is falling. For purely chronological reasons, the economic return from enabling young claimants to work is higher than the return for returning a similar proportion of older people to work. In addition, the difference between the work experience of accepted and rejected applicants aged 30 to 44 subsequent to disability determination is larger than that for older workers.[22] Furthermore, a growing proportion of SSDI applications at all ages is based on low-mortality conditions, such as lower-back pain and mental illness, where early intervention and improved incentives hold out the greatest promise for helping workers re-enter the labor force.

Conclusion

The case for encouraging those who can continue to work without undue hardship is strong. It improves their economic situation by providing earnings. If they defer claiming Social Security, they will have higher, inflation-protected, completely secure annuity income. Some research indicates that continued work is actually good for people's health. At the same time, however, many retire out of necessity or strongly felt need. No policy has been designed that flawlessly distinguishes one group from another. Thus, any policy change that saves money, in either the short or long run, will end up creating some hardship for some people. That said, a combination of measures—a selective increase in the age of eligibility for Social Security for high earners, a reduction in the age of eligibility for Supplemental Security Income together with increases in the income and asset thresholds for eligibility, and revisions in SSDI are likely to target financial assistance more accurately and promote work incentives more effectively than do current programs. As life expectancy continues to increase, the case for nudging older workers into remaining economically active will become continually stronger.

---

21. Burkhauser and Daly (2011) and Autor and Duggan (2010).
22. Wachter, Song, and Manchester (2011).

COMMENT BY
NICOLE MAESTAS

Chapter 4 provides economic analyses of several policy proposals to encourage older workers to retire later. The insightful analyses help build understanding of the potential costs and benefits associated with each proposal. The proposals, however, have different and multifaceted objectives, which makes comparison difficult. To make progress toward crafting and choosing a preferred proposal, the chapter—and we as a policy community—needs to sharpen its focus on the precise policy problem we wish to solve. A clear statement of the problem would help facilitate evaluation of the tradeoffs inherent in each proposal against a common set of criteria.

For example, is the problem that labor supply at older ages is too low (perhaps relative to some criteria)? Or is it that the disability insurance programs are imprecisely targeted and therefore labor supply among the disabled is too low? Is the solvency of the Social Security system the real issue? Or is it the federal budget deficit? Perhaps the problem is really population aging and its expected drag on economic growth. These problems are correlated, but they are not the same. Proposed solutions tailored to solve one problem can ameliorate or exacerbate the others. For instance, cutting the payroll tax might increase labor supply at older ages, but exacerbate the solvency problem by decreasing program revenues. Making Medicare the primary payer for those with employer-sponsored health insurance might increase labor demand, but increase Medicare program costs.

A sharp framing of the problem would aid us in deciding who should bear the costs of the policy solution. General benefit cuts (for example, in the form of raising the early entitlement age [EEA] or the full retirement age [FRA]) disproportionately hurt low earners. Targeted benefit cuts would disproportionately hurt high earners. Restructuring disability benefits to improve targeting could make the partially disabled worse off. Some proposals emphasize penalties, while others use rewards. For instance, is it fairer to penalize early retirement or to reward delayed retirement?

One of the proposals is to raise the EEA. If the earliest claiming age were increased by a small number of years, presumably the labor supply of people in their early 60s would also increase. As chapter 4 details, this approach generates short-term savings to the Social Security system because people would pay payroll taxes for additional years while deferring receipt of retirement benefits. A drawback of this approach is that some people may have difficulty working the additional years—people who either cannot work (because of health problems) or who cannot find work (because of labor market conditions for older workers). Postponing access to early retirement benefits would cause hardship for these groups. To the extent they claim cash disability benefits—Social Security Disability Insurance (SSDI) and Supplemental Security Income (SSI)—any cost savings would be offset.

More worrisome though is the possibility that these individuals may not qualify for SSDI and SSI. The chapter describes two possible modifications to SSDI and SSI that would facilitate their qualification for disability benefits: eliminating SSDI's recency-of-work requirement at age 62 and increasing the SSI asset and income eligibility thresholds. But this would not be enough. Fundamentally, qualification for SSDI and non-aged SSI depends on the presence of a severe health condition that will prevent work for at least a year or result in death. Although recent research shows that SSDI benefits are imprecisely targeted around the severity-eligibility threshold,[23] the standard is nonetheless stringent. An important question is thus, how many early claimants would be likely to qualify for SSDI and SSI on the basis of disability? I offer some descriptive evidence on this question in figure 4-1, which compares the health trajectories of SSDI beneficiaries to those of early claimants (those who claim retirement benefits before their FRA) over a period of fourteen years during their 50s and 60s, using data from the University of Michigan's Health and Retirement Study.[24] The four panels in figure 4-1 show how health evolves over time with respect to reporting a work-limiting health problem, self-reported fair or poor health, the number of functional limitations, and being troubled by pain. In all cases, disability insurance beneficiaries are significantly less healthy than early claimants. For example, in the bottom left panel, disability insurance beneficiaries start with more functional limitations than early claimants, and also accrue more limitations over time. Over most of the fourteen-year period, disability insurance beneficiaries (and applicants who were denied benefits) have three to four times as many functional limitations. The substantial gap between the trajectories for disability insurance beneficiaries and early claimants for retirement insurance on any of the four dimensions is notable. The health of early claimants is more comparable to that of those who claim at the full retirement age or later. These data suggest that the average early claimant would be unlikely to qualify for SSDI or SSI on the basis of health. It may indicate, however, that there is more potential work capacity among early claimants than previously thought.

In addition to deciding *what* policy should do to encourage work at older ages, it is also important to consider *how much* policy should do. The question of "how much" depends in part on what would happen if policymakers took no further action. Will labor supply at older ages continue to rise, as it has since the mid-1990s? On this point, we know more than is presented in chapter 4. The research literature suggests that a major cause of the trend reversal in labor supply in the

23. Maestas, Mullen, and Strand (forthcoming).
24. University of Michigan (2013).

Figure 4-1. *Health Trajectories by Type of Retiree*[a]

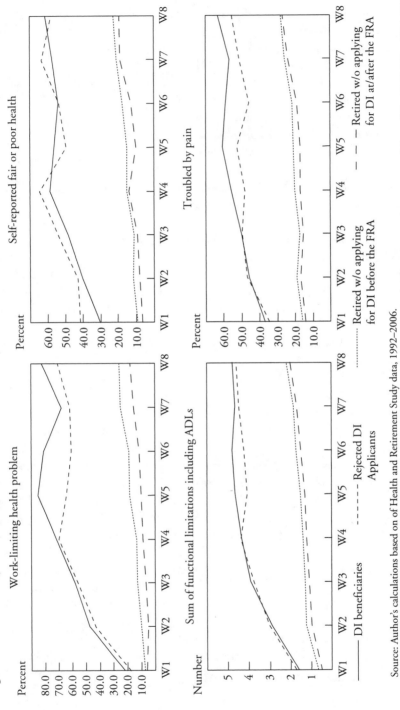

Source: Author's calculations based on of Health and Retirement Study data, 1992–2006.

a. W1, W2, and so on stand for Wave 1, Wave 2, and so on of the Health and Retirement Study. The waves translate to years as follows: W1 = 1992, W2 = 1994, W3 = 1996, W4 = 1998... W8 = 2006. ADLs = Activities of Daily Living; DI = Disability Insurance.

mid-1990s was rising education levels.[25] Technological change also played an important role by creating less physically demanding jobs. Although average education levels have since plateaued, other forces are gaining momentum.

One such force, changes in public and private pensions, is likely to drive future increases in labor supply.[26] For example, the scheduled increase in the Social Security FRA is still under way and won't be fully implemented until 2022. The restructuring of employer pensions from traditional defined-benefit schemes to defined-contribution schemes has mostly affected younger birth cohorts because a nontrivial share of defined-benefit plans were not terminated altogether, just closed to new (that is, younger) entrants. Even among terminated plans, about 95 percent have been terminations of healthy plans, in which the full value of accrued benefits was set aside to be administered by an insurer.[27] And finally, legal barriers to the use of phased retirement programs were only recently relaxed under the Pension Protection Act of 2006.

It is important to note that behavioral responses to these changes in public and private pensions that are still under way are not accounted for in most official labor supply forecasts; but they could yet turn out to be important drivers of future increases in labor supply at older ages. As a result, even if policymakers take no further action, or only modest action, these forces influencing labor supply— and other forces such as population aging that will boost labor demand—are likely to drive further increases in labor supply at older ages.

If the problem we endeavor to solve is that labor supply at older ages is too low, then we might favor policies that would change the relative desirability of retiring at different ages, and that facilitate partial retirement and labor force re-entry after retirement. The momentum behind past policy changes and behind natural forces such as population aging may mean we can be conservative in approach. However, if the real problem is system solvency, then we might favor more aggressive action in the form of policies that would reduce the desirability of retiring at *any* age.

COMMENT BY
RICHARD V. BURKHAUSER

I am the personification of the current baby boomer generation at its oldest. Born just after World War II, I have now reached the "normal" retirement age of 66. We are here and you will have to deal with us.

Rather than arguing about which metaphor to use—a scalpel or a hatchet—in thinking about how to change policy, it is better to focus on what policy changes

25. See, for example, Blau and Goodstein (2010).
26. Maestas and Zissimopoulos (2010).
27. Perun and Valenti (2008).

will be necessary to adjust the underlying factors, both demographic and economic, that have changed since Social Security was last "saved" thirty years ago with the passage of the Social Security Act of 1983. It is also important to recognize the critical role the bipartisan National Commission on Social Security played in laying out the mix of payroll tax increases and benefit reductions, including raising the normal retirement age, that became the main features of the 1983 reforms.[28] This commission—which was appointed jointly in 1981 by the U.S. Congress, with Democrats in the majority in the House and Republicans in the majority in the Senate, and a newly elected Republican president Ronald Reagan in the White House—developed a set of program changes that brought the Old-Age, Survivors, and Disability Insurance system (OASDI) into short-term balance for the next several decades. Just as important, it publicly acknowledged that long-term changes would be needed to finance the retirement of the baby boomers, given projected increases in life expectancy and the increasing ability of future workers to work past age 62. (See especially chapter 4 of the report that included Chairman Greenspan's and seven other commissioners' support not only for a gradual increase in the normal retirement age but also for a mechanism to automatically increase it in the future as life expectancy increased, beginning for those who reached age 62 in 2012.)

In thinking about the next tax and benefit changes necessary to save Social Security, it is even more important to recognize that such changes can be fashioned to alter the work behavior of older workers. But to do so in a significant way, it may prove necessary to do more than change one policy at the margin; rather, it may be necessary to simultaneously change enough policies to fundamentally change the "culture of work" for that population. That is what welfare reform legislation (especially the Personal Responsibility and Work Opportunity Act of 1996) in the 1990s did for low-income single mothers. A Republican Congress passed it and a Democratic president signed it because we decided as a society that an Aid to Families with Dependent Children program based on the notion that women should stay home and take care of their children, even if society had to subsidize them to do so, was out of step with the changing roles of American women in general. Once the majority of American women with children were working, it was appropriate to expect that single mothers do so also.

So, how did we align these policies? We made work pay for single mothers and that changed "welfare as we know it." The research community helped in this process by producing twenty years of analyses showing that with well-crafted incentives, single mothers could and would work. The individual programs that made up welfare reform in the 1990s included "carrots," such as the expansion of the Earned

28. National Commission on Social Security Reform (1983).

Income Tax Credit, extended child care for working mothers, and access to health care. But it also contained some "sticks," including time limits on welfare payments, requirement to work, and mandates on states to enforce these reforms in order to receive their block grants. Individually, each of these policies nudged single mothers to work more at the margin. But in combination, these nudges became a push.[29] The question is: Are we ready to seriously talk about reforming OASDI? I think the answer is yes. Most fundamentally it just doesn't make sense to continue to preserve an early retirement age option—set at age 62 in 1961 when the average life expectancy of 62-year-olds was 17 years—now that the life expectancy of a 62-year-old is 22 years. For couples, the average expected time until they will both be dead has risen from 25 to 29 years.[30] Given our extended lifetimes, the payments to preserve this ever-lengthening retirement option are increasingly costly to taxpayers and to society as a whole in lost productivity.

But would people aged 62 and over work if we changed incentives? That is, could they, and would they, change their behavior, if we changed the policies that have made 62 the age at which the majority of workers now take Social Security retirement benefits? I think the answer is yes, and that it would be in their interest to do so, based on the information in chapter 2. Raising the age of initial entitlement from age 62 to 65 or even pairing its increase with future changes in the age at which full benefits are paid will not save OASDI very much money. But it will have some impact on overall revenues, because these earnings will be subject to federal income tax. More important, as Burtless indicated, for most workers aged 62, it is probably in their long-term financial interest to continue to work if they are able to do so. Their wages can be used to pay for current consumption, and they will receive increased annual retirement benefits related to delaying claiming, thereby building an inflation-proof annuity that is more or less actuarially fair if taken by age 70. So, if people can work—that is, if their health allows them to work and they have jobs—it makes sense for them to do so.

It is also consistent with behavioral economics principles. Removing the early retirement option would make working past age 62 the default and in all likelihood the norm, as well as the option most likely to be in workers' best interest. Many workers who currently take the early retirement option do not fully consider the potentially negative long-term effects of doing so. Burtless mentioned some of those negative effects, but another is what happens to the survivors of workers who take early retirement benefits. Among older people, older widows now have the greatest likelihood of living in poverty, in part because their husbands took reduced benefits at age 62. Consider how much better off they would

29. See Blank (2002); Moffitt (2003); and Grogger and Karoly (2005)
30. See Steuerle (2011) for a more detailed discussion of this point.

now be if their yearly survivor's benefit were 20 percent higher back when the normal retirement age was 65. But what about when it is 25 or 30 percent higher as we further increase the normal retirement age but continue to allow workers to exercise their early retirement option at age 62?

What drives the age at which workers retire? Lots of things, but policies matter. The best documentation can be found in a series of National Bureau of Economic Research's National Institute on Aging Center on Retirement conference books focusing on the patterns of retirement in twelve OECD countries, including the United States. These studies find that average retirement age is highly correlated with the incentives in the country's national retirement programs.[31] It should not come as a surprise that social security systems that reward work up to a certain age and penalize it afterward cause workers to retire at the age when incentives change because the wealth value of their pensions falls.

Some of the changes we have made over the past thirty years have made Social Security more neutral in terms of retirement age.[32] Changes in the earnings test and increases in the bonus for delaying retirement after the age of 65 are the most notable. We now know that these policy changes mattered.[33] But they have not fundamentally changed the fact that age 62 is still the most common age to take retirement benefits.

In considering Henry Aaron's multiple-choice menu for increasing work at older ages, I would pick ending the option for workers to choose an early retirement age or, at least, to pair increases in the minimum early retirement age with increases in the normal retirement age. That should have been done in 1983 when a Democratic-controlled House of Representatives finally agreed with a Republican-controlled Senate to gradually raise to 67 the age at which full benefits are paid.

What are the possible problems with raising the early and normal Social Security retirement ages? Although most of those who are working at age 62 could continue to work, a certain percentage that could no longer take Social Security retirement benefits at age 62 would be substantially hurt, at least in the short run, by this change in policy. The good news is that only a small share of those who claim benefits at age 62 are likely to be seriously affected.[34] Using the first two years of Health and Retirement Study data,[35] my colleagues and I found that in 1993 fewer than 10 percent of males who took retirement benefits at age 62 were

31. See, for example, Gruber and Wise (1999 and 2004) and, most recently, Wise (2012).

32. Burkhauser and Turner (1978 and 1981); Burkhauser (1980).

33. See Burkhauser and Rovba (2009) for a discussion of the importance of these policy changes on work at older ages.

34. Burkhauser, Couch, and Phillips (1996).

35. The Health and Retirement Study is a longitudinal panel study that surveys a representative sample of more than 26,000 Americans over the age of 50 every two years. It is supported by the National Institute on Aging and the Social Security Administration. See Burkhauser and Gertler (1995).

both in poor health and had retirement benefits as their only source of pension income. Smith confirmed this finding using Survey of Income and Program Participation data from the same period.[36] I suspect this is still the case today.

A relatively small percentage of the population at age 62, who are not already receiving Social Security Disability Insurance or Supplemental Security Income—Disabled Adults benefits, are not healthy enough or would not have alternative retirement income sources, even if they could not access retirement benefits until later. The vast majority of these 62-year-olds are healthy enough to work, especially if they hold jobs where heavy lifting is limited. Hence, only a small minority of them are likely to be seriously harmed if, with sufficient advance notice, Social Security retirement benefits were not available until they reach the age at which the normal person is expected to work.

To put this in perspective: when my father was my age, he had been dead for four years. Most of us men will outlive our fathers and there is no reason why we cannot and should not spend at least some of those additional years working. So, what I want to do is go back to the future.

In 1977 Alicia Munnell recommended in *The Future of Social Security* separating the annuity and redistributive components of Social Security by shifting away from a strategy of providing transfer benefits to low-income older people through Social Security. We were unable to do this politically at that time. All politicians loved Social Security. Demographics were on their side, so that they could promise higher benefits without raising tax rates. Members of every age cohort got more benefits than they paid into the system because the next cohort was paying for them upfront.[37] Those golden days for Social Security are over because of declining fertility rates and growing life expectancy. Younger cohorts of workers are not likely to be willing and able to subsidize entire older cohorts of early retirement seekers in the future. Today's politicians must raise taxes, lower yearly benefits, raise the age when benefits become payable, or more likely take on a combination of all three. Raising the age of benefit acceptance and using alternative programs to protect those who are greatly harmed by this change seem the least painful way to go. Munnell recommended greater reliance on the Supplemental Security Income (SSI) system. I agreed with her then, and I agree with her now.[38]

We should take our inspiration from welfare reform and refocus Social Security to protect those people who retire at normal retirement age—age 67 or maybe even older. We should also let that age rise as life expectancy increases as Chairman Alan Greenspan and seven of his commissioners on the National Commission on Social Security first recommended thirty years ago. But we should also

36. Smith (1999).
37. See Burkhauser and Warlick (1981) for the first systematic evidence of this happy fact.
38. Burkhauser and Smeeding (1981)

recognize that this change will not solve, by itself, the long-run disconnect between promised benefits and the taxes necessary to pay for them.

Here is where some reach for the hatchet metaphor. However, I would revisit the recommendations of Republican president Bush's bipartisan Commission to Strengthen Social Security[39] that was cochaired by a former commissioner of the National Commission on Social Security Reform who had just stepped down from serving as the Democratic senator from the state of New York: Daniel Patrick Moynihan. I would shift the way we calculate the Average Index Monthly Earnings formula from a wage to a price index.[40] That shift certainly has implications. It is a reduction in promised benefits—although not in real benefit levels—as are all the previous proposals I have discussed. They are reductions because current law promises ever-increasing real retirement benefits but not the tax dollars necessary to pay for them.

Is maintaining the current system, with its automatic real-cost increases as life expectancy and real economic growth increase, sacrosanct? Could we not find more socially valuable uses for these funds? Why not expand a far more target-efficient SSI program to provide government transfers to lower-income older persons instead of automatically committing the fruits of future economic growth to ever-increasing real OASDI benefits for workers at age 62 regardless of their income or ability to work?

Currently there are two ways that adults can access SSI benefits. They must have low income and very low net worth *and* be age 65 or disabled, based on the same criteria used to establish eligibility to Social Security Disability Insurance (SSDI) benefits. But as part of a "grand compromise" in the spirit of the Social Security Act of 1983, or even better, the welfare reforms of the 1990s, why not trade off some decreases in promised future real OASDI benefit increases for an expanded role for SSI in protecting low-income older persons. One simple way to do so is to lower the age of eligibility for SSI old-age benefits from 65 to 62 and raise the SSI asset limit, while at the same time ending the early retirement age option and raising the normal retirement age.

Let me suggest why I believe such fundamental changes in the way current workers redistribute income to current older persons in the future are necessary. In a new paper, a colleague and I simulate the consequences of the projected change in the age distribution and in the share of Hispanics and African Americans in the U.S. population on the growth in median income over the next twenty years. Based on U.S. Census Bureau projections, the share of the popula-

---

39. President's Commission (2001).
40. See Cogan and Mitchell (2003) for a fuller discussion of this proposal.

Table 4-5. *Actual and Projected Average Annual Changes in Median Income from Demographic Trends, 2007–30*

	Average annual median income change accounted for by age and racial composition	
	Age	Racial composition
1979–89	0.00	–0.14
1989–2000	0.05	–0.15
2000–07	0.13	–0.29
2007–20	–0.09	–0.34
2020–30	–0.17	–0.35

Source: Burkhauser and Larrimore (2013). Authors' calculations using Public Use March CPS data and U.S. Census Bureau (2008).

tion aged 65 and over will increase from 13 percent in 2007 to 20 percent by 2030. The share of Hispanics and African Americans in the population will increase from 29 to 35 percent over the same period.

When we use a shift-share analysis, similar to the one Burtless (1999) used, and look at what accounts for changes in median income over business cycles, we find that over the 1979–89 business cycle, median income increased by 0.87 percent a year. Almost none of this increase is accounted for by changes in the age distribution, since the income of baby boomers was not much different from the average of all other age groups over that time. But because Hispanics and African Americans have lower-than-average-income, their growth as a share of the total population lowered median income by –0.14 percent a year over this business cycle (see table 4-5).

Over the 1989–2000 business cycle, median income grew by 1.11 percent a year and the baby boom generation was aging into its higher-than-average earnings years. As a result, its growth as a share of the age distribution added to median income by 0.05 percent a year, offsetting the –0.15 a year decline related to the growth of the Hispanic and African American population.

During the anemic 2000–07 business cycle, median income fell by –0.02 percent a year. But the baby boomer generation's aging into its peak earnings years accounted for a 0.13 percent a year increase that offset the –0.29 percent decline related to the growth in the Hispanic and African American share of the population.

But as the baby boom generation ages out of the labor force, the picture dramatically changes. We project that aging baby boomers will reduce median income by –0.09 percent a year, if their real incomes are the same as previous generations of

Americans aged 65 and over for the period 2007–20. At the same time, further growth in the Hispanic and African American populations will reduce median income by another –0.34 percent a year if their earnings do not increase relative to previous generations. From 2020 to 2030 these same demographic changes will account for an additional –0.17 and –0.35 percent a year decline respectively.

Demography need not be destiny, but these "no behavioral change" projections suggest that if we do not do something to increase the employment of older people as well as the real earnings of Hispanics and African Americans that will offset this straight line projection, the income of the median American will continue to grow at its current anemic pace for the next two decades. This projection is a more general reason why we should consider ending the early retirement option and increasing the normal retirement age. Finally, just as the reforms I suggest for OASI are likely to increase the employment of older workers, I believe that a substantial percentage of people who are coming onto SSDI could and would work if given the proper incentives.[41] As we think about changing the retirement system, we had better also think about changing the disability system, because those two systems are intertwined and should be considered as a whole.

COMMENT BY
DEBRA WHITMAN

My comments will reflect my current and past roles: I am now the executive vice president for policy at AARP and I previously spent ten years on Capitol Hill. When economists talk about retirement policy, it is important for them to understand how policymakers think. Having spent a lot of time with policymakers, I am going to try to present some insight on their perspective.

The overriding challenge is straightforward: If we encourage people to work longer, how do we protect those who cannot? Throughout the current recession, unemployment for older workers has been distressingly high. Today, only 38.4 percent of people 55 or older are employed. The overall unemployment rate in October was 7.7 percent, and for those over age 55, men's unemployment went up slightly to 6.2 percent and women's went down slightly to 5 percent. About 250,000 older workers have become discouraged and left the labor force. So, policymakers are bound to consider two questions: Do people want to work longer? And if they want to work longer, are there jobs for them?

First, I appreciate Henry Aaron's comments about what changing the normal retirement age really means because increases in the normal retirement age are

---

41. See Burkhauser and Daly (2011) for a fuller discussion.

really across-the-board benefit cuts. I like that Henry uses quotes around "normal," because few people wait that long to apply for benefits.

So, although increasing the normal retirement age may ever-so-slightly boost labor supply, as Joyce Manchester demonstrates, policymakers do not always understand this relationship. Raising the Social Security "normal" retirement age by one year does *not* mean that workers will continue to work another year. Joyce's figures in her comment to chapter 3 (figures 3-6 and 3-7) show that most people claim Social Security benefits at 62. For those who claim benefits at age 62, raising the "normal" retirement age means that they will live on reduced benefits for the rest of their lives.

Another key point that many policymakers miss is that while life expectancy is increasing on average, not all groups are enjoying increased longevity. Life expectancy is increasing for high earners, but not much for low earners. Life expectancy has actually declined dramatically over the last decade for people with low education—by five years for women without a high-school education.[42] Thus, if we look at policies that are based on aggregations, we have to be careful about missing the populations that are not sharing in the gains.

Similarly, there is an assumption that an increasing proportion of jobs is not physically demanding. But many jobs do remain extremely demanding especially for bodies in their mid to late 60s. So when we talk about Social Security, it is essential to keep in mind the need for fair and compassionate policies toward those who are unable to continue to work. Policymakers need to consider not just averages, but also specifics.

Without recognizing the diversity of the population, lawmakers may make policy changes that produce unanticipated or unrecognized effects. Some policymakers say that it is necessary to raise the Social Security eligibility age because life expectancy on average is increasing, but they do not account for differential mortality or health or that some jobs are more physically taxing than others. For example, the Bowles-Simpson plan contained a specific proposal to boost the eligibility age for Social Security and a slight mitigation for lifetime low-income workers, but did not include specific adjustments for workers with a disability or for those working in a physically demanding job. Chief Social Security Actuary Steve Goss computed the cost of this change. The Bowles-Simpson proposal failed to solve the problem of what to do for those who cannot continue to work—the 20 percent of the population who have work-limiting health conditions. Again, there's often a mismatch between the policies and their impact and the realities of workers' experiences.

42. Olshansky and others (2012).

Other options may be politically unacceptable because they cost too much. John Shoven's proposal in chapter 5 to eliminate the payroll tax for older workers or make Medicare the primary payer would be expensive to the respective trust funds. And even though I agree with Henry Aaron's view that SSI asset limits are too low and eligibility qualifications are too strict, the political obstacles to fixing these flaws are daunting. Why? Because in most states, once a person is on SSI, he or she becomes eligible for Medicaid. Because Medicaid costs states and the federal government, many policymakers do not want to adjust SSI eligibility and potentially increase the Medicaid costs, even though they may understand that, in principle, it would be desirable to do so.

I have a small solution. It costs nothing and I believe it is politically viable. I propose changing the name for claiming benefits at age 62 from "early retirement benefits" to something that is pejorative. Not demeaning, but faintly unsavory. Alas, I have not figured out what this new name would be. I am looking for suggestions. My point is a serious one. If one heeds the lessons of behavioral economics, how something is characterized can actually change behavior. The message should be that claiming Social Security benefits at age 62 or soon thereafter is something that people really ought not to do unless they have to. This policy would push people into behavior that is actually good for most of them, and it costs next to nothing. We would have to reprint some statements and some fliers from Social Security, but it is not much more expense than that.

I want to touch on two issues that have arisen during the fiscal cliff negotiations. One concerns a possible change in the way Social Security benefits are indexed. At AARP, we believe the shift to "chained CPI" (Chained Consumer Price Index for All Urban Consumers), a way to index Social Security benefits to the rate of inflation, or the rise in prices over time, is one of the worst ways to lower the projected long-term shortfall in Social Security. It would take a month's worth of income each year away from 90-year-olds, and they are some of the poorest people in the country. Women at age 80-plus get an average annual Social Security check of $13,000. Taking away a month's worth of benefits means cutting that average beneficiary's pension to less than $12,000. We know that few can afford such a decline when the oldest beneficiaries, those over age 75, already use 28 percent of their income for health care expenses; and they have the highest foreclosure rates of Americans 50 and older.

For reasons I described earlier, I also believe that cutting benefits by raising the full-benefits age by even a little is not worth the resulting hardships with across-the-board cuts to both low- and high-income beneficiaries.

Policymakers are also debating increases in the Medicare eligibility age. John Shoven and others have suggested that delaying access to Medicare might cause people under age 65 to work longer in their current jobs. However, it is not a viable solution with today's health insurance marketplace. When health exchanges under the Affordable Care Act are up and running and the associated tax credits are being paid, and it is clear that the limits on age-related premium differentials are implemented, it may be affordable for people under age 65 to find health care outside employment. Keep in mind that raising the Medicare eligibility age is yet another shift of risk and cost from government onto economically vulnerable groups. It is a bad idea because shifting 66- and 65-year-olds onto Medicare would increase overall health costs in the economy. Employers would pay more, Medicaid costs would go up, subsidy costs in the exchanges would increase, and those no longer eligible for Medicare would have an increase in out-of-pocket spending by over $2,000 a year.

Although many of the policy solutions currently being debated in Washington do not offer much opportunity for progress, we do need to find ways to help our society as it ages. I am pleased to say AARP is trying to help older workers find employment. AARP has begun a new initiative called Work Reimagined. We are using social networks and LinkedIn to try to help people age 50 or older get new jobs. We have commitments from 150 employers, and we are adding to those every day. The employers pledge to reach out to older workers and try and recruit them. We have a Best Employers' Program that points out workforce policies that help attract and retain older workers. And we are working with the Small Business Administration to find counseling and training for entrepreneurs aged 50-plus, already the fastest-growing group of self-employed entrepreneurs.

Finally, we are providing information to our members and anybody who visits our website to discourage them from taking Social Security retirement benefits early, and explaining the increases in the annuity value as you age.

In conclusion, I think the policy solutions regarding health care, employment, and Social Security need to be carefully designed to recognize that different groups of people have very different problems and needs. It would be unfortunate if policymakers resorted to blunt across-the-board changes that do not recognize these variations. Yes, policy should aim to increase labor force participation by older workers. It is a good thing that people are working longer, not just in bridge jobs, but in career jobs. But it is just as important to help those who lose jobs to become re-employed. As we know, it is harder for older workers than it is for younger workers to get hired. This is one of the reasons why AARP is stepping into this role.

It is also imperative to improve public understanding of the best age at which to claim Social Security benefits. For those who can afford to do so, it is usually best to live on one's own savings and delay claiming as long as possible. AARP tries to get this message across to its members.

Above all, and I think more important than anything else, we need to have an overall retirement security discussion in this country. It is important not only to make sure that Social Security can provide adequate retirement income, but also to educate people on the need to save more as life spans increase. Beyond education, it is important for public policy to encourage employers to offer workplace retirement systems so employees have an opportunity to save. I hope that the forthcoming debate on tax reform will initiate that conversation.

Table 4A-1. *Education Levels, Workers and Retirees, Age 55 through 66 (unweighted)*

Modified Question: Of those still working at age 55/58/61/62/63 and _____, what proportion retire/keep working in the next period?

Age groups and birth years	High school education or less			Some College			College degree or more		
	Retired	Still working	Obs. (no.)	Retired	Still working	Obs. (no.)	Retired	Still working	Obs. (no.)
55/56–58 (1)									
1936–37	13.0	87.0	354	12.2	87.8	98	10.1	89.9	119
1938–39	12.3	87.7	341	5.7	94.4	124	4.6	95.5	110
1940–41	10.3	89.7	271	3.5	96.6	116	9.9	90.1	131
1942–47	14.1	85.9	319	8.9	91.1	202	9.7	90.3	238
1948–52	6.5	93.5	77	6.9	93.1	87	8.4	91.6	95
58/59–61 (1)									
1936–37	16.1	83.9	286	15.7	84.3	102	9.1	90.9	99
1938–39	15.2	84.8	290	17.2	82.8	116	11.1	88.9	90
1940–41	15.2	84.8	269	12.6	87.4	135	10.7	89.3	112
1942–47	15.9	84.1	195	5.6	94.4	89	7.0	93.0	142
1948–52									
61/62–63 (1)									
1936–37	35.2	64.8	233	30.7	69.3	75	17.4	82.6	92
1938–39	33.9	66.1	230	32.6	67.4	89	20.0	80.0	80
1940–41	20.4	79.6	211	22.4	77.7	85	19.4	80.6	108
1942–47	27.6	72.4	58	23.9	76.1	46	20.4	79.6	54
62/63–65 (1)									
1936–37	27.2	72.8	195	21.3	78.7	75	21.1	78.9	71
1938–39	23.4	76.6	137	25.0	75.0	72	13.0	87.0	54
1940–41	19.8	80.2	187	24.5	75.5	94	12.4	87.6	89
1942–47	26.7	73.3	30	28.6	71.4	21	14.3	85.7	28
63/64–66 (1)									
1936–37	29.5	70.5	166	26.9	73.1	52	23.2	76.8	82
1938–39	30.3	69.7	155	32.4	67.6	71	12.9	87.1	70
1940–41	23.0	77.0	174	18.5	81.5	65	25.8	74.2	93

Source: Aaron and Callan (2011).

1. The designation "55/56–58" refers to people who were working when surveyed at age 55 and reports the indicated response when they were next surveyed, which may be when they were 56, 57, or 58; the years refer to birth years.

Table A4-2. *Impact of Health on Retirement Decisions*

Modified Question: Of those still working at age 55/58/61/62/63 and _____, what proportion retire/keep working in the next period?

Age groups and birth years	Health status			Change in health status (2)					
	Poor or fair health			Same or better			Any ADL (3)		
	Retired	Still working	Obs. (no.)	Retired	Still working	Obs. (no.)	Retired	Still working	Obs. (no.)
55/56–58 (1)									
1936–37	23.1	76.9	78	10.0	90.0	501	29.0	71.0	31
1938–39	18.4	81.6	87	7.3	92.7	482	14.3	85.7	7
1940–41	15.9	84.1	44	6.3	93.8	432	28.0	72.0	25
1942–47	22.0	78.1	82	10.1	89.9	636	25.0	75.0	32
1948–52	19.6	80.4	51	5.5	94.5	219	20.0	80.0	15
58/59–61 (1)									
1936–37	16.4	83.6	61	13.6	86.4	419	28.6	71.4	21
1938–39	29.3	70.7	75	13.5	86.5	408	32.3	67.7	31
1940–41	23.5	76.5	85	11.3	88.7	425	21.1	78.9	19
1942–47	15.5	84.5	58	8.0	92.0	350	27.8	72.2	18
61/62–63 (1)									
1936–37	27.3	72.7	77	28.4	71.6	331	42.1	57.9	19
1938–39	39.4	60.6	66	28.4	71.6	317	23.1	76.9	26
1940–41	36.4	63.6	55	17.6	82.4	318	30.8	69.2	13
1942–47	37.5	62.5	24	17.4	82.6	132	64.3	35.7	14
62/63–65 (1)									
1936–37	25.5	74.5	47	22.6	77.4	279	27.8	72.2	18
1938–39	30.0	70.0	50	19.4	80.6	211	25.0	75.0	16
1940–41	19.2	80.8	52	19.0	81.0	311	7.7	92.3	13
1942–47	18.2	81.8	11	23.2	76.8	69	0.0	100	4
63/64–66 (1)									
1936–37	43.6	56.4	39	25.3	74.7	253	28.6	71.4	21
1938–39	38.3	61.7	47	25.6	74.4	234	50.0	50.0	20
1940–41	25.0	75.0	48	21.9	78.1	260	37.5	62.5	8

Source: Aaron and Callan (2011).

1. The designation "55/56–58" refers to people who were working when surveyed at age 55 and reports the indicated response when they were next surveyed, which may be when they were 56, 57, or 58; the years refer to birth years.

2. Change in health status inquires whether health is better, the same, worse, or much worse than at the previous interview.

3. This response indicates whether respondents state they have trouble with activities of daily living: walking across a room, dressing, bathing or showering, eating, getting in or out of bed, or using the toilet.

Any functional limit (4)			Live to 75-prob. < .50 (5)		
Retired	Still working	Obs. (no.)	Retired	Still working	Obs. (no.)
12.8	87.2	399	13.7	86.3	131
11.3	88.7	284	11.0	89.0	127
12.1	87.9	231	11.2	88.8	116
12.7	87.3	355	10.6	89.4	170
11.1	88.9	117	13.4	86.6	67
17.5	82.5	240	11.3	88.7	115
18.9	81.1	259	17.8	82.2	118
15.7	84.3	281	12.7	87.3	134
11.0	89.0	219	10.1	89.9	99
33.0	67.0	212	34.3	65.7	108
32.7	67.3	220	31.1	68.9	90
24.8	75.2	214	25.3	74.7	87
27.4	72.6	84	32.4	67.7	34
28.2	71.8	188	31.2	68.8	77
25.3	74.7	150	25.8	74.2	66
21.2	78.8	222	17.9	82.1	84
19.4	80.6	36	18.8	81.3	16
26.5	73.5	170	36.4	63.6	66
32.8	97.2	177	25.4	74.7	71
26.9	73.1	182	25.0	75.0	56

4. This response indicates whether respondents state they have any difficulty with any one of the following: walking several blocks, sitting for two hours, getting up from a chair, climbing several flights of stairs, stooping, kneeling or crouching, lifting and carrying ten pounds, picking up a dime, reaching up and extending one's arms, or pushing and pulling a large object.

5. This entry shows the proportion of people surveyed who say they think the probability they will live to age 75 is less than 0.50.

Table 4A-3. *Liquid Assets*

Modified Question: Of those still working at age 55/58/61/62/63 and _____, what proportion retire/keep working in the next period?

Age groups and birth years	Up to $25,000			$25,000 to $100,000			$100,000 to $250,000		
	Retired	Still working	Obs. (no.)	Retired	Still working	Obs. (no.)	Retired	Still working	Obs. (no.)
55/56–58 (1)									
1936–37	13.3	86.7	278	12.5	87.5	152	8.3	91.7	84
1938–39	13.6	86.4	257	5.8	94.2	156	4.8	95.2	105
1940–41	8.0	92.0	238	4.7	95.3	128	11.5	88.5	87
1942–47	10.2	89.8	324	13.1	86.9	153	10.3	89.7	146
1948–52	8.5	91.5	141	0.0	100.0	36	13.3	86.7	45
58/59–61 (1)									
1936–37	13.3	86.7	195	11.2	88.8	143	20.2	79.8	84
1938–39	12.8	87.2	235	17.6	82.4	108	16.7	83.3	78
1940–41	12.3	87.7	220	12.2	87.8	115	14.6	85.4	82
1942–47	11.7	88.3	180	11.9	88.1	101	4.9	95.1	61
61/62–63 (1)									
1936–37	23.4	76.6	171	32.3	67.7	96	38.6	61.4	57
1938–39	32.5	67.5	169	29.0	71.0	100	33.9	66.2	65
1940–41	19.3	80.7	176	20.0	80.0	90	26.9	73.1	67
1942–47	33.3	66.7	57	25.8	74.2	31	25	75	28
62/63–65 (1)									
1936–37	25.5	74.5	141	19.5	80.5	77	27.8	72.2	54
1938–39	22.4	77.6	125	21.7	78.3	60	20.6	79.4	34
1940–41	21.9	78.1	160	16.3	83.7	86	18.9	81.1	53
1942–47	28.6	71.4	28	14.3	85.7	28	33.3	66.7	6
63/64–66 (1)									
1936–37	30.3	69.7	145	28.2	71.8	39	27.8	72.2	54
1938–39	28	72.0	132	30.2	69.8	63	33.3	66.7	51
1940–41	18.5	81.5	135	32.0	68.0	75	22.2	77.8	45

Source: Aaron and Callan (2011).

1. The designation "55/56–58" refers to people who were working when surveyed at age 55 and reports the indicated response when they were next surveyed, which may be when they were 56, 57, or 58; the years refer to birth years.

More than $250,000		
Retired	Still working	Obs. (no.)
12.3	87.7	57
8.6	91.4	58
14.9	85.1	67
13.2	86.8	136
2.7	97.3	37
18.2	81.8	66
15.8	84.2	76
17.2	82.8	99
11.9	88.1	84
36.4	63.6	77
25.8	74.2	66
18.1	81.9	72
11.6	88.4	43
26.1	73.9	69
20.5	79.6	44
16.4	83.6	73
23.5	76.5	17
19.1	81.0	63
11.8	88.2	51
21.8	78.2	78

Table 4A-4. *Work Conditions*

Modified Question: Of those still working at age 55/58/61/62/63 and _____, what proportion retire/keep working in the next period?

Age groups and birth years	A lot of physical effort required All or most of the time			Lifting heavy loads All or most of the time			Stooping, kneeling, crouching All or of the time		
	Retired	Still working	Obs. (no.)	Retired	Still working	Obs. (no.)	Retired	Still working	Obs. (no.)
55/56–58 (1)									
1936–37	13.6	86.4	243	11.1	88.9	108	10.9	89.1	174
1938–39	11.7	88.3	240	13.5	86.5	96	11.0	89.0	155
1940–41	9.5	90.5	179	8.1	91.9	74	10.0	90.0	140
1942–47	12.7	87.3	220	16.4	83.7	104	14.0	86.0	186
1948–52	3.7	96.3	81	2.6	97.4	38	6.7	93.3	75
58/59–61 (1)									
1936–37	15.1	84.9	205	14.5	85.5	83	14.5	85.5	131
1938–39	15.7	84.3	198	14.1	85.9	64	15.0	85.0	140
1940–41	14.9	85.1	175	11.1	88.9	72	12.7	87.3	118
1942–47	9.9	90.1	141	11.9	88.1	59	14.2	85.8	113
61/62–63 (1)									
1936–37	32.0	68.0	153	31.8	68.3	63	25.5	74.5	102
1938–39	33.8	66.2	133	31.0	70.0	42	37.1	62.9	89
1940–41	23.0	77.0	148	18.5	81.5	65	22.3	77.7	112
1942–47	30.4	69.6	46	33.3	66.7	18	27.0	73.0	37
62/63–65 (1)									
1936–37	26.8	73.2	138	31.1	68.9	45	20.9	79.1	91
1938–39	24.1	75.9	83	29.4	70.6	34	25.0	75.0	68
1940–41	19.0	81.0	116	21.1	79	57	17.2	82.8	93
1942–47	20.0	80.0	25	23.1	76.9	13	18.8	81.3	16
63/64–66 (1)									
1936–37	33.9	66.1	109	43.6	56.4	39	30.7	69.3	75
1938–39	27.1	72.9	96	36.4	63.6	33	34.9	65.2	66
1940–41	26.2	73.8	107	22.2	77.8	45	25.6	74.4	82

Source: Aaron and Callan (2011).

1. The designation "55/56–58" refers to people who were working when surveyed at age 55 and reports the indicated response when they were next surveyed, which may be when they were 56, 57, or 58; the years refer to birth years.

A lot of stress			Hours		
Agree			30+ hours/week		
Retired	*Still* working	*Obs.* (no.)	Retired	*Still* working	*Obs.* (no.)
12.9	87.1	357	9.5	90.5	495
8.9	91.2	373	8.4	91.6	514
7.9	82.1	328	7.9	92.1	455
11.6	88.4	467	10.5	89.5	685
6.9	93.1	159	5.2	94.8	231
11.6	88.4	285	12.5	87.5	417
15.5	84.5	290	13.4	86.6	418
12.3	87.7	309	11.4	88.6	446
6.8	93.2	234	9.2	90.8	369
29.1	70.9	234	29.4	70.6	323
32.2	67.8	214	29.0	71.0	317
21.1	78.95	228	20.0	80.0	325
30.8	69.2	78	24.8	75.2	121
24.8	75.2	161	21.8	78.2	248
20.6	79.4	141	18.7	81.3	198
14.8	85.2	196	15.7	84.3	268
23.7	76.3	38	23.2	76.8	56
27.2	72.8	136	27.3	72.7	209
27.3	72.7	161	21.7	78.3	203
19.1	80.9	157	17.2	82.8	233

Table 4A-5. *Pension Status*

Modified Question: Of those still working at age 55/58/61/62/63 and _____, what proportion retire/keep working in the next period?

Age groups and birth years	No pension			Only DB pensions			DB and DC pensions		
	Retired	Still working	Obs. (no.)	Retired	Still working	Obs. (no.)	Retired	Still working	Obs. (no.)
55/56–58 (1)									
1936–37	16.7	83.3	245	9.7	90.3	134	12.7	87.3	79
1938–39	11.5	88.5	226	10.8	89.2	176	6.5	93.6	62
1940–41	9.8	90.2	194	11.3	88.7	133	7.1	92.9	56
1942–47	11.2	88.8	267	11.9	88.1	168	16.8	83.2	107
1948–52	11.1	88.9	108	2.5	97.5	40	5.6	94.4	36
58/59–61 (1)									
1936–37	18.4	81.6	196	17.3	82.7	139	14.0	86.1	43
1938–39	15.8	84.2	228	18.3	81.7	115	19.5	80.5	41
1940–41	12.4	87.6	226	17.8	82.2	107	10.6	89.4	47
1942–47	16.2	83.8	173	10.5	89.5	76	5.4	94.6	56
61/62–63 (1)									
1936–37	24.4	75.6	180	41.2	58.8	85	46.7	53.3	30
1938–39	26.1	73.9	180	36.0	64.0	75	23.1	76.9	26
1940–41	20.0	80.0	190	30.7	69.3	75	17.7	82.4	34
1942–47	25.0	75.0	72	44.8	55.2	29	18.8	81.3	16
62/63–65 (1)									
1936–37	23.4	76.6	175	27.9	72.1	68	36.4	63.6	11
1938–39	19.7	80.3	137	28.6	71.4	49	30.8	69.2	13
1940–41	21.6	78.4	199	20.7	79.3	58	5.0	95.0	20
1942–47	18.9	91.1	37	40.0	60.0	15	25.0	75.0	8
63/64–66 (1)									
1936–37	23.2	76.8	164	26.7	73.3	45	31.3	68.8	16
1938–39	25.8	74.2	163	36.2	63.8	47	27.8	72.2	18
1940–41	24.9	75.1	189	39.1	60.9	46	5.0	95	20

Source: Aaron and Callan (2011).

1. The designation "55/56–58" refers to people who were working when surveyed at age 55 and reports the indicated response when they were next surveyed, which may be when they were 56, 57, or 58; the years refer to birth years.

DB = defined benefit; DC = defined contribution.

Only DC pension		
Retired	Still working	Obs. (no.)
5.1	94.9	98
5.0	95.1	101
3.4	96.6	119
8.4	91.6	190
6.0	94.0	67
3.9	96.1	103
7.5	92.6	94
10.9	89.1	119
5.9	94.1	101
23.9	76.1	88
35.6	64.4	104
12.6	87.4	95
12.8	87.2	39
17.3	82.7	75
19.3	80.7	57
14.3	85.7	77
13.3	86.7	15
32.4	67.7	68
22.4	77.6	58
10.3	89.7	68

Table 4A-6. *Individual Earnings*

Modified Question: Of those still working at age 55/58/61/62/63 and _____, what proportion retire/keep working in the next period?

Age groups and birth years	up to $6,500			$6,500 to $12,000			$12,000 to $20,000		
	Retired	Still working	Obs. (no.)	Retired	Still working	Obs. (no.)	Retired	Still working	Obs. (no.)
55/56–58 (1)									
1936–37	26.8	73.2	71	15.8	84.2	38	10.5	89.5	57
1938–39	13.8	86.3	80	21.2	78.8	33	13.3	86.7	60
1940–41	10.6	89.4	104	13.8	86.2	29	10.4	89.6	48
1942–47	13.6	86.4	147	8.7	91.3	23	16.9	83.1	65
1948–52	13.5	86.5	52	12.5	87.5	8	9.5	90.5	21
58/59–61 (1)									
1936–37	22.1	77.9	77	12.5	87.5	24	19.2	80.8	52
1938–39	19.3	80.7	114	27.6	72.4	29	7.1	92.9	56
1940–41	14.3	85.7	112	21.7	78.3	23	13.3	86.7	60
1942–47	16.7	83.3	84	5.9	94.1	17	10.3	89.7	39
61/62–63 (1)									
1936–37	28.6	71.4	91	33.3	66.7	24	19.5	80.5	41
1938–39	31.1	68.9	90	24.1	75.9	29	39.5	60.5	43
1940–41	23.7	76.3	93	32.4	67.7	34	11.1	88.9	36
1942–47	24.3	75.7	37	33.3	66.7	6	30.8	69.2	13
62/63–65 (1)									
1936–37	19.1	80.9	89	29.6	70.4	27	26.2	73.8	42
1938–39	25.0	75.0	64	7.1	92.9	14	22.2	77.8	27
1940–41	23.1	76.9	78	11.5	88.5	26	22.5	77.6	49
1942–47	25.0	75.0	20	0.0	100.0	3	0.0	100.0	4
63/64–66 (1)									
1936–37	20.9	79.1	86	29.2	70.8	24	29.4	70.6	51
1938–39	26.9	73.1	93	38.5	61.5	26	26.7	73.3	30
1940–41	27.3	72.7	99	42.4	57.6	33	16.2	83.8	37

Source: Aaron and Callan (2011).

1. The designation "55/56–58" refers to people who were working when surveyed at age 55 and reports the indicated response when they were next surveyed, which may be when they were 56, 57, or 58; the years refer to birth years.

$20,000 to $40,000			$40,000 to $75,000			More than $75,000		
Retired	Still working	Obs. (no.)	Retired	Still working	Obs. (no.)	Retired	Still working	Obs. (no.)
7.8	92.2	179	11.5	88.5	165	9.8	90.2	61
8.2	91.8	170	7.9	92.1	164	1.5	98.6	69
6.6	93.4	136	8.2	91.9	135	7.4	92.7	68
10.5	89.5	162	8.3	91.7	218	12.5	87.5	144
4.6	95.5	66	6.3	93.8	64	4.2	95.8	48
11.7	88.3	145	15.0	85.0	133	7.0	93.0	57
8.9	91.1	124	17.9	82.1	112	14.5	85.5	62
12.5	87.5	136	10.8	89.2	120	16.9	83.1	65
13.3	86.7	98	9.2	90.8	120	4.4	95.6	68
39.2	60.8	125	27.5	72.5	80	20.0	80.0	40
29.0	71.0	107	31.0	69.1	84	29.8	70.2	47
18.2	81.8	88	19.8	80.2	101	18.9	81.1	53
22.7	77.3	44	30.3	69.7	33	15.4	84.6	26
34.9	65.1	86	17.0	83.1	59	21.1	79.0	38
24.4	75.6	82	14.0	86.0	57	31.6	68.4	19
15.5	84.6	110	20.6	79.4	68	19.5	80.5	41
15.4	84.6	13	28.6	71.4	28	27.3	72.7	11
29.4	70.6	68	34.9	65.1	43	24.1	75.9	29
20.3	79.7	64	30.9	69.1	55	20.7	79.3	29
16.7	83.3	66	18.6	81.4	59	18.0	82.1	39

Table 4A-7. *Total Household Income*

Modified Question: Of those still working at age 55/58/61/62/63 and _____, what proportion retire/keep working in the next period?

Age groups and birth years	Up to $15,000			$15,000 to $25,000			$25,000 to $40,000		
	Retired	Still working	Obs. (no.)	Retired	Still working	Obs. (no.)	Retired	Still working	Obs. (no.)
55/56–58 (1)									
1936–37	31.3	68.8	32	11.8	88.2	51	10.1	89.9	79
1938–39	16.2	83.8	37	12.9	87.1	31	11.4	88.6	79
1940–41	19.2	808	26	3.5	95.6	29	8.6	91.4	58
1942–47	18.8	81.3	32	9.5	90.5	42	12.1	87.9	66
1948–52	10.0	90.0	20	19.1	81.0	21	4.6	95.5	22
58/59–61 (1)									
1936–37	26.9	73.1	26	13.3	86.7	30	12.7	87.3	71
1938–39	15.8	84.2	38	6.7	93.3	30	11.9	88.1	67
1940–41	17.2	82.8	29	10.8	89.2	37	18.6	81.4	70
1942–47	25.0	75.0	20	24.0	76.0	25	10.0	90.0	50
61/62–63 (1)									
1936–37	42.1	57.9	19	33.3	66.7	30	28.6	71.4	77
1938–39	31.3	68.8	32	19.2	80.8	26	33.3	66.7	54
1940–41	40.0	60.0	25	21.9	78.1	32	22.2	77.8	54
1942–47	42.9	57.1	14	27.3	72.7	11	33.3	66.7	24
62/63–65 (1)									
1936–37	29.2	70.8	24	27.3	72.7	33	25.5	74.6	55
1938–39	22.2	77.8	18	22.2	77.8	18	30.0	70.0	40
1940–41	20.8	79.2	24	30.4	69.6	23	14.1	85.9	64
1942–47	33.3	66.7	3	14.3	85.7	7	0.0	100.0	7
63/64–66 (1)									
1936–37	44.4	55.6	18	32.3	67.7	31	25.5	74.6	55
1938–39	40.0	60.0	15	33.3	66.7	24	31.6	68.4	57
1940–41	47.8	52.2	23	25.0	75.0	28	13.7	86.3	51

Source: Aaron and Callan (2011).

1. The designation "55/56–58" refers to people who were working when surveyed at age 55 and reports the indicated response when they were next surveyed, which may be when they were 56, 57, or 58; the years refer to birth years.

$40,000 to $60,000			$60,000 to $105,000			More than $105,000		
Retired	Still working	Obs. (no.)	Retired	Still working	Obs. (no.)	Retired	Still working	Obs. (no.)
12.6	87.4	103	11.2	88.8	169	10.2	89.8	137
13.5	86.6	119	6.9	93.1	174	5.2	94.9	136
10.0	90.0	100	6.9	93.1	159	8.8	91.2	148
12.7	87.3	126	10.7	89.3	234	10.4	89.6	259
5.3	94.7	38	5.1	94.9	78	7.5	92.5	80
10.1	89.9	89	16.5	83.5	152	14.2	85.8	120
21.9	78.1	96	11.0	89.1	137	17.1	83.0	129
9.8	90.2	92	12.4	87.6	145	14.7	85.3	143
12.9	87.1	70	9.7	90.3	124	6.6	93.4	137
30.0	70.0	70	36.4	63.6	110	21.1	79.0	95
35.7	64.3	84	33.0	67.0	112	25.0	75.0	92
23.8	76.3	80	16.8	83.2	101	15.9	84.1	113
27.8	72.2	18	27.0	73.0	37	12.7	87.3	55
27.6	72.4	58	21.4	78.6	98	23.3	76.7	73
8.5	91.5	47	27.7	72.3	83	17.5	82.5	57
20.3	79.7	69	18.4	81.6	98	19.2	80.9	94
12.5	87.5	16	35.0	65.0	20	26.9	73.1	26
20.8	79.3	53	30.4	69.6	79	23.1	76.9	65
22.2	77.8	54	28.6	71.4	70	19.5	80.5	77
25.8	74.2	62	17.5	82.5	80	23.6	76.4	89

References

Aaron, Henry J., and Marie Callan. 2011. "Who Retires Early?" Chestnut Hill, Mass.: Center for Retirement Research at Boston College (May 12).

Atkinson, A. B. 2012. "The Mirrlees Review and the State of Public Economics." *Journal of Economic Literature* 50, no. 3: 770–80.

Autor, David, and Mark Duggan. 2010. "Supporting Work: A Proposal for Modernizing the U.S. Disability Insurance System." Washington, D.C.: Center for American Progress and the Hamilton Project.

Behncke, Stefanie. 2009. "How Does Retirement Affect Health?" Discussion Paper 4253. Bonn, Germany: Institute for the Study of Labor (IZA).

Blank, Rebecca M. 2002. "Evaluating Welfare Reform in the United States," *Journal of Economic Literature* 40, no. 4: 1105–66.

Blau, David, and Ryan Goodstein. 2010. "Can Social Security Explain Trends in Labor Force Participation of Older Men in the United States?" *Journal of Human Resources* 45, no. 2: 328–63.

Bound, John, and Timothy Waidmann. 2007. "Estimating the Health Effects of Retirement." Paper prepared for the Ninth Annual Joint Conference of the Retirement Research Consortium, August 9–10.

Burkhauser, Richard V. 1980. "The Early Acceptance of Social Security—An Asset Maximization Approach." *Industrial and Labor Relations Review* 33, no. 4: 484–92.

Burkhauser, Richard V., Kenneth A. Couch, and John W. Philips. 1996. "Who Takes Early Social Security Benefits: The Economic and Health Characteristics of Early Beneficiaries." *The Gerontologist* 36, no. 6: 789–99.

Burkhauser, Richard V., and Mary C. Daly. 2011. *The Declining Work and Welfare of People with Disabilities: What Went Wrong and a Strategy for Change.* Washington, D.C.: American Enterprise Institute Press.

Burkhauser, Richard V., and Paul J. Gertler, eds. 1995. "The Health and Retirement Survey: Data Quality and Early Results." *Journal of Human Resources* 30 (Special Issue, December).

Burkhauser, Richard V., and Jeff Larrimore. 2013. "Accounting for United States Median Income Inequality Trends over the First Decade of the 21st Century and Beyond." Working Paper. New York: Russell Sage Foundation.

Burkhauser, Richard V., and Ludmila Rovba. 2009. "Institutional Responses to Structural Lag: The Changing Patterns of Work at Older Ages." In *Aging and Work*, edited by Sara J. Czaja and Joseph Sharit, pp. 9–34. John Hopkins University Press.

Burkhauser, Richard V., and Timothy M. Smeeding. 1981. "The Net Impact of the Social Security System on the Poor." *Public Policy* 29, no. 2: 159–78.

Burkhauser, Richard V., and John A. Turner. 1978. "A Time Series Analysis on Social Security and Its Effects on the Market Work of Men at Younger Ages." *Journal of Political Economy* 86, no. 4: 701–16.

———. 1981. "Can Twenty-Five Million Americans Be Wrong? A Response to Blinder, Gordon and Wise." *National Tax Journal* 34 (December): 467–72.

Burkhauser, Richard V., and Jennifer L. Warlick. 1981. "Disentangling the Annuity and Redistributive Aspects of Social Security in the United States." *Review of Income and Wealth* 27 (December): 401–21.

Burtless, Gary. 1999. "Effects of Growing Wage Disparities and Changing Family Composition on the U.S. Income Distribution." *European Economic Review* 43, no. 4–6: 853–65.

Coe, Norma B., and Maarten Lindeboom. 2008. "Does Retirement Kill You? Evidence from Early Retirement Windows." Discussion Paper 3817. Bonn, Germany: Institute for the Study of Labor (IZA).

Coe, Norma B., and others. 2010. "The Effect of Retirement on Cognitive Functioning." Unpublished paper. Chestnut Hill, Mass.: Center for Retirement Research at Boston College (December).

Cogan, John F., and Olivia S. Mitchell. 2003. "Perspectives from the President's Commission on Social Security Reform." *Journal of Economic Perspectives* 17, no. 2: 149–72.

Dhaval, Dave, Inas Rashad, and Jasmina Spasojevic, "The Effects of Retirement on Physical and Mental Halth Outcomes." Working Paper 12123. Cambridge, Mass.: National Bureau of Economic Research (March).

Goss, Stephen C. 2010. "Choosing to Work During Retirement and the Impact on Social Security." Testimony to Committee on Finance, United States Senate, July 15.

Grogger, Jeffrey, and Lynn Karoly. 2005. *Welfare Reform: Effects of a Decade of Change.* Harvard University Press.

Gruber, Jonathan, and David A. Wise. 1999. *Social Security and Retirement around the World.* National Bureau of Economic Research Book Series. University of Chicago Press.

———. *Social Security Programs and Retirement around the World: Micro-Estimation.* National Bureau of Economic Research Book Series. University of Chicago Press.

Gustman, Alan L. and Thomas L. Steinmeier. 2012. "Behavior Effects of Social Security Policies on Benefit Claiming, Retirement, and Saving." Ann Arbor: Michigan Retirement Research Center, University of Michigan (August).

Kahneman, Daniel, and Amos Tversky. 1979. "Prospect Theory: An Analysis of Decision under Risk." *Econometrica* 47, no. 2: 263–92.

Kerwin Kofi Charles. 2002. "Is Retirement Depression? Labor Force Inactivity and Psychological Well-being in Later Life." Working Paper 9033, Cambridge, Mass.: National Bureau of Economic Research (July).

Kirk, Adele. 2012. "Understanding the Growth in Federal Disability Programs: Who are the Marginal Beneficiaries, and How Much Do They Cost?" Working Paper 2012-1. Chestnut Hill, Mass.: Center for Retirement Research at Boston College.

Leonesio, Michael V., Denton R. Vaughn, and Bernard Wixon. 2003. "Increasing the Early Retirement Age under Social Security: Health, Work, and Financial Resources." Brief No. 7. Washington, D.C.: National Academy of Social Insurance (December).

Liebman, Jeffrey B., and Jack A. Smalligan. 2013. "An Evidence-Based Path to Disability Insurance Reform." Paper presented at a Brookings Institution conference, Washington, D.C., February.

Maestas, Nicole, Kathleen Mullen, and Alexander Strand. Forthcoming. "Does Disability Insurance Receipt Discourage Work? Using Examiner Assignment to Estimate Causal Effects of SSDI Receipt." *American Economic Review.* August 2013.

Maestas, Nicole, and Julie Zissimopoulos. 2010. "How Longer Work Lives Ease the Crunch of Population Aging." *Journal of Economic Perspectives* 24, no.1: 139–60.

Moffitt, Robert A., ed. 2003. *Means-Tested Transfer Programs in the United States.* University of Chicago Press.

Munnell, Alicia H. 1977. *The Future of Social Security.* Brookings Institution Press.

Munnell, Alicia H. 2012. "Can the Actuarial Reduction for Social Security Early Retirement *Still* Be Right?" Working Paper 12-6. Chestnut Hill, Mass.: Center for Retirement Research at Boston College (March).

Munnell, Alicia H., and Steven A. Sass. 2007. "The Labor Supply of Older Americans." Working Paper 2007-12. Chestnut Hill, Mass.: Center for Retirement Research at Boston College (June).

Myerson, Noah, and Joyce Manchester. 2012. "Raising the Ages of Eligibility for Medicare and Social Security." Blog post, Congressional Budget Office, Washington, D.C., (January).

National Commission on Social Security Reform. 1983. *Report of the National Commission on Social Security Reform.*

OECD (Organization for Economic Cooperation and Development). 2009. *Pensions at a Glance, 2009: Retirement-Income Systems in OECD Countries.* Paris.

Olshansky, Jay, and others. 2012. "Differences in Life Expectancy due to Race and Educational Differences Are Widening, and Many May Not Catch Up." *Health Affairs* 31, no. 8 (August): 1803–13.

Perun, Pamela, and Joseph J. Valenti. 2008. "Defined Benefit Plans: Going, Going, Gone?" Paper presented at the Thirtieth Annual Association of Public Policy Analysis and Management Research Conference, Los Angeles, November 7.

President's Commission to Strengthen Social Security. 2001. *Social Security and Creating Personal Wealth for all Americans* (December).

Report of the National Commission on Social Security Reform. 2003. *Social Security Bulletin* 46, no. 2: 1–38.

Rohwedder, Susan, and Robert J. Willis. 2010. "Mental Retirement." *Journal of Economic Perspectives* 24, no. 1 (Winter): 119–38.

Salhgren, Gabriel H. 2012. "Work 'til You Drop: Short- and Longer-Term Health Effects of Retirement in Europe." Working Paper 928. Stockholm: Research Institute of Industrial Economics (IFN).

Schultze, Charles. 1977. *The Public Use of Private Interest.* Brookings.

Shoven, John, and George Shultz. 2008. *Putting Our House in Order: A Guide to Social Security and Health Care Reform.* New York: Norton.

Shoven, John B., and Nita Nataraj Slavov. 2012. "The Decision to Delay Social Security Benefits: Theory and Evidence." Working Paper 17866. Cambridge, Mass.: National Bureau of Economic Research (February).

Smith, Ralph. 1999. "Raising the Earliest Eligibility Age for Social Security Benefits." Congressional Budget Office Paper (January).

Steuerle, Eugene. 2011. "The Progressive Case against Subsidizing Middle-Age Retirement." *The American Prospect* (February).

University of Michigan. 2013. *Growing Older in America: The Health and Retirement Study.* Survey and database supported by the National Institute on Aging and the Social Security Administration (http://hrsonline.isr.umich.edu/).

U.S. Census Bureau. 2008. *US Population Projections: National Population Projections* (www.census.gov/population/www/projections/downloadablefiles.html).

Wachter, Til von, Jae Song, and Joyce Manchester. 2011. "Trends in Employment and Earnings of Allowed and Rejected Applicants to the Social Security Disability Insurance Program." *American Economic Review* 101 (December): 3308–29.

Waldron, Hilary. 2007a. "Trends in Mortality Differentials and Life Expectancy for Male Social Security–Covered Workers, by Socioeconomic Status." *Social Security Bulletin* 67, no. 3: 1–28.

———. 2007b. "Mortality Differentials by Lifetime Earnings Decile: Implications for Evaluations of Proposed Social Security Law Changes." *Social Security Bulletin* 73, no. 1: 1–37.

Wise, David A. 2012. *Social Security Programs and Retirement around the World: Historical Trends in Mortality and Health, Employment, and Disability Insurance Participation and Reforms.* National Bureau of Economic Research Book Series. University of Chicago Press.

5

Thoughts on Working Longer and Retirement

JOHN B. SHOVEN

Let me start by questioning whether people really are working to older ages today than they were twenty years ago or that properly computed age-specific labor force participation rates have gone up over the same period. To return to an old theme of mine,[1] it depends on how you measure age. The remaining life expectancy of the average retiree has not gone down over the past twenty years. The mortality of people at retirement has not gone up. The average duration of retirement has increased, not fallen. So, in a very real sense people are not working to "older ages." I recognize when people say that people are working to older ages, they mean that the average retiree is older using the conventional years-since-birth measure. But while retirees today are further from birth than they were twenty years ago, they are also further from death. If you are further from death, you could legitimately be considered to be younger. This perspective calls for a reexamination of how we measure age. It also calls into question the premise that people are working to older ages.

The issue of adjusting policies for longer lifetimes is one of the biggest tasks for public policy over the next twenty to thirty years. Let us review a couple facts about demographics and real interest rates. A recent study shows that the average retirement age for men has risen to 64 and the average retirement age for women has risen to 62.[2] What is the remaining life expectancy of a 64-year-old man married to a 62-year-old woman? Rather than report their individual life expectancies, I will report the expected time until both spouses have died: that is, how long a second-to-die annuity would have to make payments. Based on the Social Security

1. Shoven (2004, 2010).
2. Munnell (2011).

cohort life tables with intermediate assumptions from the Social Security Administration's 2012 Trustees Report,[3] the answer is 27.38 years for the average couple. If they were at the 75th percentile of the time until the second death, then the second death would occur after 31.5 years; at the 90th percentile, after 35 years. Insurance companies are well aware that life annuity purchasers have better-than-average life expectancy. They would price a joint life annuity with the expectation of at least 30 years of payouts.

What were the corresponding numbers in 1961, the first year that workers were given a choice as to when to commence Social Security? At that time, the average retirement age for men was 66, not 64. Although the retirement age has crept up lately, it still is two years below where it was fifty years ago. A 66- and 64-year-old couple (preserving the assumed two-year age difference) retiring in 1961 had an expected time to second death of 21.05 years, 6.33 years less than now. The remaining life expectancy of the average retiring couple has increased by 30 percent since 1961. My guess is that people underestimate how long their retirement resources need to last and that many of us underestimate how much longer retirements have gotten.

Let's assume that the couple wants a retirement income of 75 percent of their preretirement income. Abstracting from Social Security (that is, assuming that they were going to have to come up with all of the funds privately), how much wealth would they need to have accumulated? Today, a reasonable real (safe) discount rate is zero (using Treasury Inflation-Protected Securities [TIPS] rates for reference), so to keep their real income constant, they need 75 percent of 27.38 years, or 20.53 times their annual preretirement earnings. In 1961 it would have been reasonable to use the 2.9 percent real interest rate assumed by the Social Security Trustees, so the wealth multiple would have been 21.05 times 75 percent times an annuity factor reflecting the real interest earnings on the unspent balance during the annuity period. Doing the simple mathematics gives a required balance that is 11.69 times preretirement income. Rounding off, the retirement wealth needed today is 20.5 times annual earnings. In 1961 it was 11.7 times earnings. Today's figure is 75.6 percent higher! About half of the higher cost of providing for retirement is due to longer retirements and half is due to lower interest rates.

How long would a typical couple age 64 and 62, have worked? A reasonable maximum is about forty-five years, but forty years seems more realistic. The question is: Is it possible to finance a twenty-seven-plus-year retirement with a forty-year career? Would this work for a defined-benefit plan, a defined-contribution

3. Board of Trustees (2012).

plan, Social Security, or any other plan or combination of plans? My answer is no, or at least not without a distinctly un-American level of savings. For this reason, I think that the trend toward later retirement has only just begun. I believe that by 2050, by which time life expectancy will almost certainly have increased four or five more years, the average retirement age will be at least 70. That is the only way to make the pension mathematics work.

Policy changes are needed to remove disincentives toward working longer. I have written about two policies with coauthors Sita N. Slavov and Gopi Shah Goda (2007, 2009, 2011) and in a 2008 book with George P. Shultz. First, establish a new class of worker whom we call "paid up." The idea is that after forty years of contributing to Medicare and Social Security, this worker is paid up and could work additional years with no payroll tax for either the employee or the employer. Ending the payroll tax for these workers would increase their take-home pay and lower employment costs for their employers. These changes would encourage those with long careers to keep working and their employers to retain them.

Second, end the policy under which Medicare is the secondary payer after private employer-sponsored health insurance and replace it with one with Medicare as the primary payer. Today we have a policy that offers those 65 and over a valuable national health insurance benefit unless they work for an employer with twenty or more employees that offers a health insurance plan, in which case Medicare benefits are pulled back and the employer and employee have to pay for health insurance themselves. This policy discourages work past age 65. If Medicare were the primary payer, workers would receive Medicare benefits whether or not they worked, and the employer and employee would be responsible for no more than a Medigap policy. It would significantly increase the return to working.

Sita Slavov and I[4] find that almost all people file for Social Security as soon as they can: at 62 or as soon as they retire. They then use their private assets such as 401(k) accounts to supplement Social Security. This almost universal practice is a big mistake for most people. Private assets should be used not to *supplement* Social Security, but rather to *defer* Social Security. The return to deferring Social Security is not determined by market forces; it is determined by legislation. That return is outstanding, fabulous, and way above the market. For example, if you wait until age 70 to claim Social Security benefits, your real monthly benefits will be 76 percent higher than if you claim at age 62. The lifetime value of the gain from deferring depends on whether you are married or single and, if you are married, whether you are the higher or the lower earner. But some deferral is optimal for just about everyone. We even find that people with twice the average mortality rates (smokers, for

---

4. Shoven and Slavov (2012a and 2012b).

instance) should defer benefits somewhat. Single males with twice the average mortality should not claim benefits until age 65 and single females with twice the average mortality should wait to 68. The cumulative lifetime value of waiting until the optimal claiming age, rather than claiming at age 62, can be more than $200,000. People are leaving a lot of money on the table. Early claiming instead of optimal claiming particularly hurts widows and widowers.

COMMENT BY
STEVEN PEARLSTEIN

I'm not an economist. Actually, I don't teach in the economics department at George Mason. As you can imagine, they wouldn't have me. I'm in the government department. And I'm not an actuary. So, a lot of the tables and data in this volume make my head hurt. What follows is the reaction of a journalist.

I turned 61 two weeks ago, and I'm very happy to know that 61 is the new 54.

First, I will make a small nonacademic point. John Shoven assumes that because the Treasury Inflation-Protected Securities (TIP) rate is zero, the discount rate is zero. I don't think that when real people in the real world think about their retirement savings, they think that their rate of return is zero. They can invest in a broad portfolio of dividend-paying blue-chip stocks and earn 2 to 3 percent. They can also put their money into the Wellesley Income Fund at Vanguard and, over a long period, be pretty sure that they are going to earn in excess of 5 percent. So, I don't really think that's the way real people think about their discount rate.

A lot of John's chapter has to do with how much incentive or disincentive we are giving people to continue to work or not continue to work. I'd like to start out with a basic and obvious point. In the 1930s and then in the 1960s we decided, as a matter of social policy and because we felt it was fair and because we wanted some economic security, to create programs called Social Security and Medicare. These programs are inherently disincentives to working. So, we shouldn't be surprised that there are disincentives for older people to work. We set it up that way, not because we wanted to maximize GDP, but because we felt better about the overall outcome. We liked it. It was what we wanted to do. Initially we set up a small intergenerational transfer that has now become a huge intergenerational transfer, because we set the programs up as pay-as-you-go systems.

John and others point out that because of the tax and benefit system in these two programs, we've created marginal tax rates that are now a further disincentive for older people to work. According to John, this requires another round of intergenerational transfers in order for us to solve the problem. He suggests that we let people who work beyond 65 do so without a payroll tax and let them dip into

Medicare earlier even while they're working, essentially raising the cost to both programs, which are already heading toward insolvency.

It seems to me that we are on a slippery slope here. We are just piling on one more intergenerational transfer to solve a problem created by a previous set of intergenerational transfers. If you worry about those sorts of things, as I do, then I think we probably want to call a stop to it.

John's chapter also raises a philosophical question. Is the lack of an incentive a disincentive? And whenever there is a lack of incentive or disincentive, should the government step in and solve that problem?

For example, when you talk about somebody being "paid up" in terms of Social Security, that sounds nice. But is the program actually paid up? Well, not really. None of us, as far as I know, ever really fully pays for our Social Security or Medicare benefits. So we're not really paid up. I think that's a misnomer, and I am uncomfortable if we pay even less.

John commented extensively about the incentive effects of implicit marginal tax rates on older workers, and about how such incentives change their behavior. It seems to me that implicit in these observations is the assumption that people are "foresightful" and rational and that we are well-informed, income-maximizing economic actors. In other words, it is assumed that we act like economic models say we are supposed to act. If so, these high-implicit marginal tax rates are bad because they discourage us from working.

But John also described some very important work that he has done on the best time to claim benefits under the current rules. He has shown that most of us make a huge mistake when we decide to claim Social Security at age 62 and that we are all leaving a lot of money on the table, up to $200,000 over a lifetime, which is roughly $6,500 a year. It seems hard to me to reconcile these two visions of how we behave. Do you believe that we respond very aggressively to implicit marginal tax rates? Or are we all silly and leave money on the table? Either we are silly or we are rational, but we can't be both at the same time.

Henry Aaron has pointed out an obvious problem that I don't consider huge, but John's solutions—"Medicare first" and the payroll tax holiday—will weaken the solvency of those two programs. As Gary Burtless and Gene Steuerle pointed out, people working and generating income longer will generate more money for the U.S. Treasury through their income taxes. But that is a separate pocket of money unless we want to figure out a way to transfer income tax revenue back into the Social Security and Medicare systems. Then we have a political problem.

I'd like to deal briefly with something Gene Steuerle wrote in his response to chapter 3. He said we don't have to worry about the demand problem for all the additional labor from older workers. The reason is that the decline in birth rates during a certain period of time means that there will be sufficient demand for labor and that it won't affect unemployment of other people. I'm not sure how much we can count on that. To a degree, of course, but it is not axiomatic that supply will create its own demand as it did when women came into the workforce or when immigrants came, or when there was a technology change and suddenly there were excess workers because of productivity increases.

I think that in a global economy where wages and prices are sticky and institutional arrangements favor insiders versus outsiders, it is not necessarily true that labor supply everywhere always creates its own demand. We have all seen microexamples and anecdotal information. Long-time youth unemployment and underemployment have been persistent problems in major industrial countries over long periods of time. The system doesn't necessarily clear. I don't exactly know why; each country is a little bit different, but I don't think it is necessarily true that old people who continue to work will not take jobs from unemployed young people, at least not in the short and the medium term.

At the micro level, I think we all work in places where we know that if we were to retire, our employers would hire somebody younger and cheaper. So, at the micro level, we have at least anecdotal evidence that there would be some displacement. Those of us who have young-adult children know that many are in the inevitable, unending, unpaid internship phase of their careers. The system is not exactly working for the 20-somethings, even those with good educations.

In response to whoever cited Standard & Poor as saying we were coming to full employment in either 2017 or 2018, I would be very happy to take the other side of that bet. Economic forecasters always say that after some number of years the system will clear and return to equilibrium, to full employment. They always say that; they are programmed to say that. But there is really no reason to believe it is true. In fact, we know that there are structural problems in our labor markets that contribute to high unemployment today and will cause us to have high unemployment in 2017.

It seems the best argument is the simplest one, which John made. You can't have forty-five years of work pay for thirty years of retirement in a slow-growing economy where retirement savings are less than 20 percent of your income. That's just math. I don't even think that's economics—its arithmetic—and it is a problem.

I tend not to focus on the macro stuff as much as on the micro stuff. My father-in-law just celebrated his 90th birthday. He's a federal judge on senior status. Three times a week he gets up at 6 o'clock in the morning to go ice dancing. It seems to me that the reason he has lived so long is because he worked longer—working longer is a good thing for reasons that go beyond macroeconomics.

I think the reason people decide to retire or not to retire is not primarily driven by policy. There are all sorts of other things: how much money they have, how happy they are with their job, whether their spouse works, whether their kids live nearby, whether they have a house or cottage at the lake that they own and can go live in. There are all sorts of reasons why people decide to retire when they do, and I'm not sure I think it's the role of government to worry about this or try to use policy to affect it. I also think the decision to retire is largely driven by the employment policies in the workplace. Some places are more flexible and make transitional arrangements whereas others do not. That is probably an area we ought to think about more than policy change.

My last conclusion is that, to a surprising degree, markets are working. If Gene Steuerle is right, we can expect at least a gradual increase in demand for work from older workers. We know that labor supply by the elderly is increasing. We know that the wages of older workers are increasing, and that the retirement age is starting to rise again. It looks to me as if the market is working pretty well. I am not sure why we have to do anything to solve the problem. There is not necessarily a policy solution to every problem. Perhaps the best policy is neutrality. If so, we shouldn't be encouraging or discouraging retirement at any particular age. We should simply keep as neutral a policy as we can.

GENERAL DISCUSSION

HENRY AARON: I want to push a little harder on the two suggestions that John Shoven made for policy changes involving the fully paid-up Social Security worker and Medicare as a primary payer. First, the Social Security proposal, at least, would heavily favor men relative to women, given the fact that women tend to have relatively short working careers.

Second, these proposals are, in a fundamental way, incomplete. They cost resources. Certainly within the individual trust funds of the programs, they deepen already existing deficits in the Medicare Hospital Insurance Trust Fund and in the Old-Age, Survivors, and Disability Insurance Trust Fund. Whether they deepen an overall budget problem is a closer question in light of the possible impact it would have on potential GDP and revenue collections. At least in the near term, they are very likely to deepen that problem as well. To make the proposal complete, you have to combine it with how you pay for it within the trust funds and within the overall budget. Then you need to make the case that this is how we should use scarce resources—and budget resources are surely quite scarce just now. Should we provide an additional benefit or tax relief heavily slanted toward men rather than women, and that is going to have to be paired with some other things that aren't so much fun to do.

John, the floor is yours.

JOHN SHOVEN: I'm not sure I can definitively answer these points. Let me start with the discount rate. If you are eligible for Social Security—say you are 62 or over and you have worked for more than ten years—I think we all agree you have an asset. You have a U.S. Treasury–backed asset that will pay you monthly checks for the rest of your life. That asset is inflation indexed. You have a Treasury-backed, inflation-indexed asset. Your security happens to be a life annuity and not a bond, but it's very close to a Treasury-backed, inflation-protected security—a TIPs bond. In valuing such an asset, what discount rate should you use? You should use the rate of return paid on assets like the one you have: TIPS. Now, could you use a higher discount rate, such as the return on a stock mutual fund? In that case, you would be using a rate of return on a risky asset, not a rate of return on a safe asset. I'm claiming that one should use the rate on safe assets, which is a zero real interest rate. Current rates of return on safe assets today are actually below zero. No money market fund is offering even a zero real rate of return. They are paying negative real interest rates. No bank is offering a positive real rate on savings deposits. So, anyway, I claim that you don't want to use a risky discount rate to discount a safe asset.

On the two policies—the paid-up Social Security worker idea and the Medicare as primary payer idea—one should think about how the government as a whole would fare, not how one part of the government—the trust funds—will fare. I don't think we are claiming necessarily that people calculate their implicit tax rates. All we are claiming is that older workers respond to their paychecks—that is, to net wages. I am not claiming that 45-year-olds are very responsive to wages. They are going to work anyway. When you're in your 60s, work is more optional. Estimates by Eric French indicate that the labor supply of older workers is quite elastic. If they are paid more, they work more. We did a back-of-the-envelope calculation indicating that Medicare as a primary payer would not cost the U.S. government anything because the extra income tax would exceed the losses to Medicare.

We can't settle whether the government should look at all its sources of revenue and the overall budget, or at each trust fund and make sure that no policy harms that trust fund. Just to be clear, Medicare would obviously be paying more benefits. Medicare's financial situation would be worse. At the same time, the Internal Revenue Service would be collecting more income taxes.

As to whether men will benefit more than women from paid-up Social Security because men are more likely than women to have a forty-year covered earnings record, that's true; but many retirees are married. With a couple, the distinction in income between the man and the woman is blurred. Also, many widows are collecting on the earnings record of their deceased husbands, not their own. So, the gender roles get blurred.

Even single retirees can often claim on an ex-spouse's record. One strategy in efficient retirement design is to claim your spousal benefits from your ex-spouse or claim your survivor benefits from your ex-spouse, all the while deferring your own record. At age 70, if the benefit based on your own earnings is higher, you switch to your own record. But for those first years, you are actually collecting on somebody else's record. Certainly there are lifetime single women, but they are probably not having the career interruptions for child rearing and so forth. Although this needs further investigation, I think that many people have two claims to work with, one for a man's record and one for a woman's record. It might not be as much of a concern as it appears.

The thing that we have to sort out is this issue of whether we worry about the trust funds per se or whether we worry about the government's budget. Perhaps we worry about both. What I am claiming is that these policies would not necessarily worsen the government's overall budget problem. They may worsen the trust funds, and you will have to figure out whether that is something that can be fixed.

AARON: Before we open it up for comments or questions, I want to mention research that bears on whether anyone has paid fully for his or her Social Security. Dean Leimer at the Social Security Administration did a study some years ago showing that some age cohorts have paid for their benefits and some have not. Cohorts born before about 1935 have not paid fully for their Social Security benefits. Cohorts born later have paid fully for their benefits. Within each cohort, there are high and low earners, couples and single people, and the ratio of taxes to benefits differs for these groups. But if you average across everybody in an age cohort, people born since around 1935 have paid for their benefits. That is progressively more true for more recent cohorts.

SHOVEN: Let me emphasize one point. A lot of people are working on issues such as discount rates that local governments should use for evaluating the financial status of their pension funds, and about the timing of claiming, and about the relative incentives of defined-benefit versus defined-contribution pensions and about the details of Social Security reform. But the big question that overshadows everything is that it is hard to see how one can finance thirty-year retirements with forty-year careers. I referred earlier to forty-five-year careers, but the average retiree does not have a forty-five -year career. How one finances thirty-year retirements with forty-year careers is a bigger problem than all of these other issues.

ELI GREENBLUM: I am an actuary. Professor Shoven, I agree with basically everything you said. Your comments about the difficulty of paying for a thirty-year retirement with a forty-year career are absolutely true. The American Academy of Actuaries is trying to push for the legislators to change the Employee Retirement Income Security Act of 1974 (ERISA), which now prohibits branding a retirement age greater than 65 as the normal retirement age. We actuaries would like Congress to authorize plans to brand a higher normal retirement age, at least to align with Social Security's full retirement age.

STEVE PEARLSTEIN: I'm not telling you as an actuary what discount rate you should use when making calculations for whatever it is you make calculations for. What I'm saying is that if you are talking about the discount rate people use in making decisions about what they want to do and when they retire, they don't think they are going to be earning zero on their money. You should ask what they perceive their discount rate to be, not what you know the rate is based on the current yield on TIPS. That rate is dominated by institutional investors looking for places to park money, not by individuals wondering about how they're going to pay for their retirement.

SHOVEN: Steve, I don't disagree, but I would add that the average person is thinking of nominal, not real interest rates. They think about nominal interest rates. So, our assumption of a 0-percent real rate corresponds to 2-percent nominal rate.

GARY BURTLESS: I want to turn the discussion back to something that Steve mentioned earlier— the assumption of full employment in the long run. That is, it is assumed that if older workers want to join the workforce, the private market will create the employment opportunities for them to do so. Steve points out, correctly, that for long periods this situation has not been true. If the situations in Spain in 2012, Greece in 2012, Europe 1980 to 1995, and the United States from 1929 to 1940 mean anything, they certainly mean that there can be too little demand for people to work for very long periods.

My point is that most U.S. neoclassical economists are strongly inclined to think unemployment is a short-run problem and in the long run, if people want to work, employment opportunities are going to be created for them. I am putting myself in that group. Still, in our modeling for this project, we did not assume that there was instantaneous market clearing. We assumed that there would initially be a lot of extra unemployment. We made various assumptions of alternatives about where that unemployment would occur—just among the aged or shared with the non-aged. But we do think that, looking at the long record in the United States, by and large, eventually policy gets things approximately right. Over long periods, certainly more than ten or eleven years, we assume that problems of unemployment will be resolved. I would like to hear the counter argument to that view. What evidence exists over long periods of time in a country like the United States to show a shortfall in the willingness of employers to create employment opportunities for everybody—whether they are women, minorities, or aged people?

PEARLSTEIN: I can't go toe to toe on this with you economists. I just would ask you to observe what is happening in this country. I realize this is not Spain and Greece, and it's not Europe and that we have much more flexible labor markets. But we can observe that for a lot of groups, wages have gone down here and that there are pockets of structural unemployment that are very real. They don't go away as quickly as we would like or as our models said they would.

For a long time, economists have said that immigration has little or no effect on wages or employment. I think we now know that immigration does have an effect on wages and, I would argue, that over many years and for many people, especially those with little education, immigration can have some pretty serious effects on unemployment. So, from a political standpoint if nothing else, you want to be careful about saying we need to encourage as many old people as possible to stay in the workforce when we have a lot of 20-somethings including 20-somethings with college degrees who are unemployed and underemployed. It is not a fanciful problem.

SHOVEN: Steve, I don't think you and Gary necessarily disagree. I think, Gary, you are saying that in the short run unemployment will increase if the number of elderly who want to work increases, that in the long run wages will be lower, and that lower wages is what will make the market clear. Right?

BURTLESS: That's what I think.

MARLENE LEE: I work at the Population Reference Bureau as a demographer. David Wise has done a cross-national study on the displacement effect of employment of older persons on youth employment. He found that there was no displacement effect.

SHOVEN: I think the story behind that finding has got to be much along the lines that Gary described. In the short run, if there is excess supply and you add further to the supply, you are going to make unemployment rates higher. But over periods long enough to allow even relatively rigid labor markets to gradually adjust, it is capacity limitations that determine how far demand policy can go. For most periods when the economy is at or near full employment, if you expand the labor supply pool, you also expand capacity to produce and, very likely, actual output as well.

PEARLSTEIN: Let me pose just two little wrinkles. I believe that over the next fifteen years we are going to have macroeconomic fiscal drag from efforts to cut the structural budget deficit. That is one thing affecting aggregate demand. Although older workers may be earning extra income, their propensity to spend these marginal dollars may well be lower than that of an average middle-aged worker. If so, the share of their earnings that the elderly consume will be smaller than if those same earnings had gone to younger workers.

I'm just posing all sorts of qualifications to the neat little model of the labor market where everything always eventually comes out right. I am obviously not questioning that a lot of women went to work and somehow we got to be a richer economy because of it. And we got a lot of immigrants and they found work too. But it isn't always so smooth and easy.

SHOVEN: As another example, recall that the baby boom hit the labor market around 1970. The impact was delayed a bit by the Vietnam War, particularly for men. But in the short run, the economy had some problems and wages were depressed a bit, as the labor market digested the baby boomers.

RICHARD BURKHAUSER: Yes, I would like to look at this issue from another angle. In looking at the unemployment rate as a key parameter, I note that policymakers have a tendency to reduce the unemployment rate, not by increasing employment but by giving people an alternative way to be not unemployed. Those knowledgeable about the history of the Social Security system know that in 1936 removing the unemployed from the labor force was one of the major reasons why people supported a Social Security system. The law said that people lost all their benefits if they worked at all, even earning $1. So, we have to be careful of the notion that we are going to use the disability program or the old-age program to hide unemployment. There is a cost to that in the sense that eventually these people can and should work. If they do, they will increase GDP.

SHOVEN: I'm just calling for a policy of neutrality. I'm not trying to encourage anyone to work or discourage anyone from working.

EUGENE STEUERLE: I have a question for John Shoven and Henry Aaron. I think that the debate you are having may be the wrong debate. I suggested Medicare as a secondary payer back twenty years ago. So have a lot of others. It seems to me these changes are matters of horizontal equity. We are saying the system is unfair because it is not providing equal justice for people who have the same lifetime earnings but very different benefits. John is proposing a fix to improve fairness in order to promote employment. Henry says that it might cost the system something. And John replies that it probably will not. But isn't the point that if there are horizontal inequities we should fix them?

AARON: I would like to point out the radical political implications of John's Medicare proposal. The root argument is that treating health insurance as part of the compensation package distorts either the supply of or the demand for labor. He proposes basically to take it out of that calculation, but only for workers over age 65. Well, if the principle that including health insurance in compensation distorts labor markets, one should want to remove that distortion for workers at all ages. That calls for a completely different method of health insurance coverage in the United States from one where health insurance is tied to employment. So, if one wants to take quite seriously the principle that John has articulated, he should be favoring Medicare for all.

SHOVEN: Hank, the idea can't be that radical, because the policy I described was actual policy for eighteen years. From 1965 to 1983 Medicare was the primary payer for everyone eligible for the program.

DEBRA WHITMAN: John, your estimate of how much the coming generation will need in retirement was huge. But you were just looking at replacing previous earnings. You left out rising health care costs, and in particular long-term care costs. The average nursing home now costs $100,000 a year. How can we incorporate that into estimates of what people will need for retirement?

SHOVEN: I think Debra is saying that my assumption that retired people need only 75 percent of what they had when they were earning might not be right. They might need more than 75 percent, particularly the very elderly who need nursing homes services. That strengthens my point that you can't finance those last thirty years of life with forty years of work. We might have to go back to twenty-year retirements, which is about where we were fifty years ago.

STANFORD ROSS: I was a Social Security commissioner and the only one who actually reformed the disability program, maybe the only one who ever will. That is a bridge to the comment I want to make. I did a paper a few years ago examining all the incentives in the law for early retirement. There was never a coherent policy discussion. They were all one-off amendments from some Ways and Means or Senate Finance Committee member to deliver a bauble, a benefit. They add up to produce a system tilted towards early retirement. If we could get to neutral, that would be pretty good, much less to a system that encourages later retirement. It would take a lot of legislative engineering to do that. That brings me to my agreement with John Shoven.

The big problem is that it is almost impossible to adapt the institutions anymore. We have not seen a major reform of the tax system or the Social Security system in a long time. Ideology seems to be replacing policy analysis and evidence. The big issue going forward is whether the political system will allow us to adapt the institutions that we have, whether we will get a tax system and a Social Security system that would be more suitable than what we have now.

What is your judgment, John? You have identified this as up there with extreme weather and climate change as problems that demand attention.

SHOVEN: Before you can get to reform, you need a general understanding of the problem. How long did it take to lead up to the 1986 tax reform? Ten or fifteen years. A good first step would be if people understood the commonality between the bankruptcies of several cities in California and the problems of southern Europe. Ridiculous retirement ages are a common element. Once we realize that retiring at 55 if you are going to live to 90 is just nuts, we might begin to change it.

AARON: I'd like to pick up on the issue of neutrality, which various people have made. Steve Pearlstein is foursquare for neutrality, but what exactly does neutrality mean? David Wise and Jon Gruber answered that question in the first of their major international comparative studies of retirement systems. They defined a concept called "retirement force" in the retirement systems. Fundamentally, the question is: For a worker, does the retirement system raise or lower the net wage that you receive for an additional year of work? You pay taxes, but you acquire some additional benefit rights, so those offset one another at least in part. What they found was that in a number of European countries, the implicit tax rate was enormous. You worked, you got a wage, but the net wage after allowing for taxes and retirement benefits was a small fraction of your stated wage. In the United States the retirement system was almost exactly neutral. So if you are a neoclassical economist who believes that people perceive exactly the incentives to which they are exposed and react to them, we have neutrality. Now, I don't think that anything material has happened in the years since they did this study. If anything, I suspect, it has tilted a bit toward favoring continued work, because increased longevity has increased the lifetime value of incremental retirement benefits.

So, if one says the U.S. system isn't neutral, one must be invoking things other than the neoclassical indicators of how the system affects people's behavior. You have to be invoking liquidity constraints. People may really want to quit work but are unable to do so because they don't have the cash until they reach age 62 and become eligible for Social Security. That may be why you see the retirement spike at that age. I just think it is very important to be clear on what we mean by nonneutrality. Nonneutrality, I think, is qualitative access, a characterization of what normal behavior ought to be, but it is not the inherent economic incentives in the retirement programs. So, a lot of what's being talked about goes back to the observation that maybe we could find a way of making early retirement just uncool, unchic.

Richard Burkhauser has emphasized that reforms in the structure of disability insurance could go a long way toward helping people return to work if they are given the right services at the right time, if employers were motivated in the right way to help them do that. There are really big opportunities for gain. But I don't think that is the sense in which we are using the terms neutrality or nonneutrality.

SHOVEN: There is a big exception, Henry. Traditional defined-benefit plans remain important for state and local workers and remain important for many private sector workers. They have the same old incentives for early retirement— if you work beyond the normal retirement age. However, they have diminished in coverage and importance and, in all likelihood, they will diminish further. I think most of us regard this loss of the incentive to retire as a step forward.

BURTLESS: I would go further, Hank. Let's go back to the time when there was one retirement age: 65. If you deferred retirement after that, there was no adjustment in your benefit. If you earned anything at 65 you were prohibited from collecting a pension. That was one extreme. By the time that David Wise and John

Gruber did their book, we had a relatively neutral public pension system. From the point of view of neoclassical economists looking at that, it's neutral.

STEUERLE: Medicare is not neutral.

AARON: I was going to get to Medicare in one second. Medicare is the route to an affordable group insurance for those over age 65. Only at age 65 do people gain access to an affordable group health plan outside employment. It's called Medicare. That will change in 2014, when the Affordable Care Act and health exchanges come into effect.

BURTLESS: Let me try to summarize this discussion. Most of us recognize that with increasing life expectancy, the twentieth-century trend to earlier and earlier retirement had to end. It seems to have done so. People are retiring later than they did just twenty years ago. John Shoven has made a strong case that this trend to longer working lives should continue because the implied tax and saving rates if life expectancy continues to increase and retirement ages do not increase look insupportable. Our empirical estimates show that a continuation of recent trends toward later retirement would increase federal revenues and reduce federal spending. Cumulatively these changes could directly reduce federal borrowing by roughly $4 trillion over the next three decades. Reduced interest payments on a smaller federal debt would cut debt even more. Those savings are not sufficient to close future budget deficits under the more pessimistic projections of the Congressional Budget Office. But they help. Furthermore, Gene Steuerle makes a good argument that increases in labor-force participation may be larger than commonly recognized because employers will seek to keep older workers on the job to offset the dwindling ranks of younger workers.

It is important to recognize that the United States has come a long way from the days when both private and public pensions made it very costly for people to continue working past the age at which pensions were initially available. Our pension system—Social Security and 401ks—now provides larger pensions to those who defer claiming them. Policy changes can abet those trends, as Henry Aaron and Rich Burkhauser observe, by raising the age of initial eligibility for Social Security and reforming Social Security Disability Insurance. But as Debra Whitman and Steve Pearlstein stress, great care needs to be taken to meet the needs of those for whom continued work is difficult or impossible.

References

Board of Trustees. 2012. "The 2012 Annual Report of the Board of Trustees of the Federal Old-Age and Survivors Insurance and Federal Disability Insurance Trust Funds." Washington, D.C.: Social Security Administration.

Goda, Gopi Shah, John B. Shoven, and Sita Nataraj Slavov. 2007. "A Tax on Work for the Elderly: Medicare as a Secondary Payer." Working Paper 13383. Cambridge, Mass.: National Bureau of Economic Research, September.

———. 2009. "Removing the Disincentives in Social Security for Long Careers." In *Social Security Policy in a Changing Environment*, edited by David A. Wise, Jeffrey Brown, and Jeffrey Liebman. National Bureau of Economic Research. University of Chicago Press.

———. 2011. "Implicit Taxes on Work from Social Security and Medicare." In *Tax Policy and the Economy*, National Bureau of Economic Research. University of Chicago Press.

Munnell, Alicia H. 2011. "What is the Average Retirement Age?" Policy Brief 11-11. Chestnut Hill, Mass.: Center for Retirement Research at Boston College (August).

Shoven, John B. 2004. "The Impact of Major Life Expectancy Improvements on the Financing of Social Security, Medicare and Medicaid." In *Coping with Methusaleh: The Impact of Molecular Biology*, edited by Henry Aaron. Brookings.

———. 2010. "New Age Thinking: Alternative Ways of Measuring Age, Their Relationship to Labor Force Participation, Government Policies and GDP." In *Research Findings in the Economics of Aging*, edited by David A. Wise. University of Chicago Press.

Shoven, John B., and George P. Shultz. 2008. *Putting Our House in Order: A Guide to Social Security and Health Care Reform*. New York: Norton.

Shoven, John B., and Sita Nataraj Slavov. 2012a. "The Decision to Delay Social Security Benefits: Theory and Evidence." Working Paper 17866. Cambridge, Mass.: National Bureau of Economic Research (February).

———. 2012b. "When Does it Pay to Delay Social Security? The Impact of Mortality, Interest Rates and Program Rules." Working Paper 18210. Cambridge, Mass.: National Bureau of Economic Research (July).

Contributors

HENRY J. AARON
Brookings Institution

RICHARD V. BURKHAUSER
Department of Policy Analysis and
    Management, Cornell University, and
    Melbourne Institute of Applied Economic
    and Social Research, University of
    Melbourne

GARY BURTLESS
Brookings Institution

RICHARD W. JOHNSON
The Urban Institute

NICOLE MAESTAS
Center for Disability Studies,
    The Rand Corporation

JOYCE MANCHESTER
Congressional Budget Office

STEVEN PEARLSTEIN
George Mason University and
    The Washington Post

JOHN B. SHOVEN
Stanford Institute for Economic Policy
    Research, Stanford University

KAREN E. SMITH
The Urban Institute

STEVEN PEARLSTEIN
George Mason University and
    The Washington Post

EUGENE STEUERLE
The Urban Institute

DEBRA WHITMAN
AARP

Index